Praise for The Field of Boaz!

In the tapestry of biblical love stories, the narrative of Boaz and Ruth stands as a timeless testament to the beauty of relationships woven with faith, integrity, and grace. As a shepherd and spiritual father to many, I am delighted to present this book by my son, Pastor Ukporhe Austin. It delves into the rich fields of Boaz and Ruth, harvesting the seeds of wisdom planted in their extraordinary love story. Just as Boaz saw the virtuous character in Ruth amidst the fields, this book invites you to glean insights that transcend time and culture. May the gleanings from Boaz and Ruth's relationship serve as a harvest of inspiration for your own journey of love and companionship. Through the pages of this book, let the legacy of Boaz and Ruth as well as the life experiences of Pastor Austin guide you to fields where love blossoms and relationships flourish under the watchful eye of our providential gardener, Jesus Christ. God bless you.

Rev & Rev Mrs Felix Meduoye
Convener and President of Grace Life Ministries, Former General Overseer of Foursquare Gospel Church, Nigeria.

....

The Field of Boaz is a wonderful script, an intricately woven tapestry of the biblical story from the book of Ruth and the journey of the life of God's servant, Rev. Austin. In sublime fashion, lessons emerge naturally from the convergence of stories, and the delightful plot twists all backed up by the rich heritage of scripture that the book rests on. This work will give light to many seekers and grant wisdom to all who encounter it. I absolutely recommend it. Congratulations to Rev. Austin Ukporhe on this magnificent work.

Rev. Gideon Odoma
Fortress Ministry, Jos.

When it comes to writing, an author is faced with the arduous task of effectively conveying the message in their heart onto the pages of a book, leaving no room for confusion. When this task is successfully accomplished, everyone will attest and say, 'This book is excellent!' We must say that Rev. Austin has succeeded in doing just that. His choice to blend personal life stories, valuable lessons, and biblical wisdom from the story of Ruth and Boaz couldn't have been better expressed. As a couple who have had the privilege of counselling many in the relationship and marriage scene, we understand how much amplification godly wisdom for marriage needs in this age and time. So we must say that this book is a breath of fresh air, offering answers to many of the questions that trouble young, unmarried men and women on their journey towards wholeness and readiness for marriage. Rev. Austin has poured his heart onto the pages of this book, and we can already foresee the blessing it will be to those who read it with open hearts ready to learn. This is a must-read!"

Reverend Ohis and Anwinli Ojeikere (The Winlos)

....

This is a well-crafted book that masterfully weaves the life of Rev. Austin Ukporhe and his pilgrimage so far into anecdotes and archetypes encoded by biblical personalities. It tells us how our human realities and experiences are counterfoils of men and women who experienced the grace of God and thereby found transformation, meaning and satisfaction in Christ Jesus. Rev. Austin shows unequivocally that our present and future seem to have a prophetic interpretation and or correlation in the stories of heroes of faith. A highly relatable book, it encapsulates the many-sided weaknesses and erennial problems that bedevilled a generation of champions that grace called out of darkness into God's blazing glory. It connects the reader to our common humanity and shared societal failures and the rescuing power of God's love to those who would surrender to divine help through Christian discipleship processes. In this treatise, Rev. Austin gives us a window into his journey and calling while boldly inviting us into the endless possibilities available in walking with Jesus. It is my hope that every reader will respond to the eloquent challenge of a deeper walk of grace echoed through the pages of this book. I strongly recommend this to everyone who wants more of God and a life of meaning.

Morakinyo Olumodimu (Ph.D Tulane)
Senior Pastor, The Upward Church.

Clarskville, Maryland, USA.

....

The Field of Boaz is a masterpiece. The mercy and grace of God in divine election is a palpable reality of the Kingdom of God. This is expressed so beautifully in this book with the parallels of the story of Naomi and Ruth together with the experience of the writer, showing the unending benevolence of God towards His people. Naomi had suffered untold pain after departing Bethlehem (the house of bread), in search of bread with her husband. Still, it was from this pain, that Ruth, a Moabite, a people of abomination before God, became a partaker of the mercy of God. Being a descendant of Lot from inception, Ruth was engrafted into the lineage of Jesus by God's mercy alone. Recall how God showed great mercy to Lot the father of the Moabites in the days of the destruction of Sodom and Gomorrah. Despite Lot's departure from His grace, God preserved him and even after, God remembered his descendants, allowing them to have an inheritance in Christ through the person of Ruth. Knowing this, the book takes us through a practical experience of how the mercy of God can search out men regardless of their circumstances, deliver them from the power of darkness and convey them into the Kingdom of His dear son, our Lord Jesus Christ. In this hope, we are comforted, that no matter how hard we have fallen, His mercy can always bring us back home, settle us in all areas of life and grant us goodness. The lessons on marriage presented in the book are profound and inspiring. All these can only come from a diligent scholar like Rev. Austin Ukporhe.

Prophet Ayo Jeje
Serving Overseer, Prophetic Streams

....

Foundation is critical to everything in life. In this book, Pastor Austin did an incredible job laying out a practical approach to choosing a life partner. It is a must-read for teenagers, young adults, and anyone who is seeking to have a godly marriage. Personally, I like how Pastor Austin used his personal experience, selecting his life partner, to relate to how Boaz and Ruth established an eternal union that led to the genealogy of our Lord Jesus Christ. As you read the book, I will draw your attention to Chapter Seven, where Pastor Austin outlined some characteristics of what a man and a woman should look for in their future partner.

Akin Ayemobola (San Antonio, Texas),
Pastor & Finance Executive in a Fortune 25 Company in the United States.
....

The decision of the writer to be brutally naked and vulnerable with his life experiences, the faithfulness of God through those experiences, and a sound teaching from the bible to show and teach that God is indeed love, and He doesn't use our mistakes against us makes this book more relatable to an everyday Joe than most Christian books I've read in the last few years. This is a must-read bestseller in the making.

Femi Akioye
MD/CEO Channeldrill Resources Ltd.

....

The best book is not the one written in fiction or illusions; the best of books are those written in men. The life of Reverend Austin is not just a book like some others, his life journeys and experiences can be termed bestsellers. I have known Reverend Austin for close to three decades. He has penned down his own life. Take my words to the bank that what you have is the experience of a man transformed by the very hand of God Almighty. For lack of apt and succinct descriptive adjectives and metaphor, permit me to use a self-made but Yoruba-inspired metaphor to describe this spiritual yet aesthetically well-sculptured and woven masterpiece (The Field of Boaz by Ukporhe J. A). This piece is a "Gbogbonishe," that is, a single solution for multiple challenges. Austin has intellectually and spiritually, prepared a dose in this semi-autobiographical book to heal and immunize marital relationships of three categories: the magnificent marriages, those that are managing theirs as well as a solution for those in misery. The yet-to-be-married have even more to learn from this masterpiece. This thirteen chapter book expresses a prototypical experience of the life of a Moabite by the name of Ruth. A. J. Ukporhe tells his own story in style as he compares his life-crushing experience with the ungodly background of Ruth as he links the line with her ancestor-Lot. I love the artistic craftsmanship and prowess shown by Austin from chapters six to thirteen. I call that the map for a successful journey from courtship into a successful marriage life. Most youths these days can't have a holy and healthy relationship life due to factors attributable to a kind of civilization that is alien to the Christian culture. I am very sure that those who purchase and consume the contents of this book will stand out both in life and in destiny. According to George R.R. Martin "A reader lives a thousand lives before he dies; the man who never reads lives only one." So have a nice reading experience.

Rev. Dr. Ben Audu Musa
The State Chairman, Pentecostal Fellowship of Nigeria (PFN),
Sokoto Chapter, and the State Pastor CHC, Sokoto, Nigeria.

A must-read book for a contemporary generation whose definition of relationship is constantly being redefined by the world. The author, the book and the message are a triune blessing that was well woven together by God Himself in this book. The author, Reverend Austin's childhood is the first dose of blessing in this book. How the great and magnificent one (Augustine/John) whose future is great (Okiotodoro) but was temporarily a Bature and notoriously an outlaw now became an apostle, only God could weave such an intricate destiny together even from birth. His early childhood abuse by his Aunty Anna is a reminder to our present-day parents to keep an eye on our children and protect them from the Aunty Anna and Uncle Anna under our roof. I love the comparative analogy of Ruth and Austin in the book. It brought the scripture to light and made it real. His willingness to be led by the Holy Spirit in his choice of a marital partner is a practice that we are losing in the church today. Reverend Austin's testimony in this book is proof that God still gives spouses like he did for Adam and that inter-tribal marriages can work if brought under the authority of our Lord Jesus Christ. I have no doubt that this book will bless parents, mostly fathers. Thank you, Reverend Austin, for allowing yourself to be vulnerable in God's hands in writing this epistle. God bless you.

Obafemi George
CEO Barachel Realty Limited.

....

The Field of Boaz is a book that should not just be read but studied. In these times where accurate discipleship before and post marriage is lacking in the body, this book is an effective discipleship tool that should be read by singles, intending and married couples. Furthermore, the book clearly delineates and inadvertently gives concrete meaning to 1st Corinthians 1:26-29. "For you see your calling Brethren, not many nobles, not many wise in the flesh and not many mighty are called...but He uses the foolish things of this world to confound the wise." The writer's salvation story succinctly captures God's redemptive work for man after the fall through the death and resurrection of Jesus Christ, blended with an accurate exposition of God's intention for marriage using the premarital journey of Ruth and Boaz. It is important to note the parallels between Ruth and the writer, who seemed to be nothing before they accepted God's way and path. They were transformed to become pillars in the agenda of God for the redemption of Israel and the body of Christ respectively.

Charles Ugbegbua
Investment Banker, New York, USA.

....

Scripturally sound and spirit-charged, this is one of the most helpful books providing practical theology on finding and sustaining Christian relationships that will lead to marriage. Ukporhe's ability to stay in the present day while referencing the past, and prophetically unveiling the future makes this a much-needed book offering a biblical road map for real hope, and the promise of supernatural joy and fulfilment in marriage for those who genuinely desire Godly relationships. Every church leader and sanctified Christian should read this book.

Kesiena Esiri
(RCN Warri)

....

Reverend Austin, a distinguished servant of God and a cherished friend and brother, masterfully weaves the tapestry of his life's narrative remarkably. He courageously juxtaposes the complexities of his own past, which we could humbly refer to as 'ugly,' with one of the most profound biblical stories of grace, mercy, divine favour, and divine direction - the story of Ruth and Boaz. This book serves as a compelling testament to the ever-present grace of God and the enduring potential for transformative change in the lives of all individuals. There is so much it covers - Relationship, Repentance, Reconciliation, Revival, Restitution and Restoration - to mention a few. Reverend Austin's storytelling is both accessible and profound, deeply enriched with biblical truths. As you read, get ready for an encounter with the Spirit

of the Living God!
Godwyns Ade' AGBUDE [Ph.D]
Leadership Expert, Political Theorist, Filmmaker and Global
Missionary. Chief Executive Director, GODWYNS AGBUDE
STUDIOS LLC, CALIFORNIA, USA

....

This book is a treasure trove filled with virtue that has been squeezed from the life of a man who has yielded to the mighty hand of God. It is not one of those cleverly crafted fables that is embellished with fluffy claims and textured in the similitude of a high fantasy. It is the substantive testimony of a man saved, pruned and anointed by Jesus for a generation. From a background that could best be described in two words, mazy mess; in the most unlikely of places on earth, the parched plains of the Sokoto Caliphate of Nigeria, mercy has once again said, NO! And grace has yet again intensified its salvific capacities to deliver and commission – even God's prophet, Austin Ukporhe! I have had the rare privilege of reading this book. It is an effective weapon against the heavy-duty cosmic attack against the institution of marriage. Singles and married alike will definitely find it useful.

Rabeeu Nas Madaki
Chief Scribe, Iron Pen Kalma Kraft Ltd, Lafia,
Nasarawa State, Nigeria.

....

Rev. Austin in his book, The Field of Boaz, with the wisdom of God, explored the word of God in the area of singleness and marriage. He dissected the book of Ruth coupled with his own experience on the issue of making the right choice in marriage. He makes it clear that it is possible for anyone no matter how spiritual, to get it wrong and emphasises the need for patience when it comes to knowing the will of God. Using the book of Ruth and his own life experience, he reiterates that it is possible to have a successful marriage regardless of your past mistakes. The patterns and the methods of the world will not suffice. There is a need for wisdom and guidance from the Lord. Rev. Austin highlights the importance of understanding and embracing the fact that God wants to guide our every step, this however, requires surrendering to the wisdom of the Lord instead of trusting our own human understanding. God is all-knowing and has the best plan for our lives. "For I know the thoughts that I think toward you, says the Lord, thoughts of peace and not of evil, to give you a future and a hope." (Jeremiah 29:11 NKJV). "I know what I'm doing. I have it all planned out - plans to take care of you, not abandon you, plans to give you the future you hope for" (Jeremiah 29:11 MSG). Rev. Austin makes it clear in his book that it is important that we prioritise hearing the voice of God and faithfully act on the promptings of the Holy Spirit even if it contradicts how one feels. Marriage, a unique institution, as it is, was ordained by God. It is not a traditional human arrangement. When we acknowledge this and God's intention for marriage, our focus will be shifted from self-reliance towards God's leading and providence. I strongly recommend this book for everyone, single and married. Be abundantly blessed.

Dr (Mrs) Funmi Alawale
God's Vineyard Ministries, UK

....

One phrase to describe the book, The Field of Boaz, will be "from streets to palace!" This is a story of a complete one-eighty turn in the life of Austin, a young boy who was abused from age seven, grew up into being highly promiscuous, picked up several vices from the streets and practically grew into being a don in the hoods! The Field of Boaz is a book of God's redemptive grace. It demonstrates the similitude between Ruth's vindication from her past, as compared by the author, and the boy, Austin's journey to God. "On September 14th, 1999, I hopped on a motorcycle, heading to Tudun Wada to meet the guys as usual. But that day, the feeling of emptiness that had been haunting me returned with a vengeance." The atypical way the Lord stirs up the work of redemption in the life of humans is one that will forever remain puzzling. Austin's journey of salvation demonstrates God's inexplicable love and how He orchestrates a pathway back to Him irrespective of our involvement. He comes searching even when we are completely clueless. Written with the execution mindset of a bible reading journal, I particularly enjoyed the action points at the end of each chapter giving room for self-reflection and specific steps to take. The Field of Boaz tops my list of recommended books, particularly for someone who is constantly battling with the feeling of inadequacy and a haunted past. It's a book that speaks of true love and marriage despite all odds. Furthermore, it reminds us of the eternal love of God our Father.

Kemi Okusanya
CEO, Hydrogen Payments
(a Subsidiary of Access Corporation), Lagos, Nigeria.

THE FIELD OF BOAZ

Austin J. Ukporhe

THE FIELD OF BOAZ

Published under permission in Nigeria by the Publishing Arm of:
Life Spring Global Resources.
Head Office: 21, Baale Street, Boundary-Ajegunle, Apapa,
Lagos, Nigeria.Tel: +234 8136616635, +234 9099331577.

Email: lifespringresources@gmail.com.

**Names of certain individuals mentioned in this book have been changed where
anonymity is deemed necessary to protect the**

honour and image of the individuals involved.

THE FEILD OF BOAZ, Nigeria.
Life Spring Global Resources.

DEDICATION

To my wife, Ebunoluwa (ER), because you are God's 'Grace' to me, and my field that keeps blooming.

ACKNOWLEDGEMENTS

I would like to acknowledge the input from various influences in my life for this book and express my appreciation to those who collaborated with me. My profound gratitude goes to my spiritual father, Apostle Arome Osayi, and his wife, Rev. Dinna Osayi, for their biblical insights that have inspired and shaped me into the person I am today. I extend my thanks to my friend and brother, Rev. Gideon Odoma, for his substantial contributions to the revision of the manuscript. Thank you for being there right from the start.

I am especially grateful to my parents, without whom I would not be here today. You were the perfect parents God prepared to raise a son like me. I am glad your later years were better than the former, and now you rest in the presence of the Lord.

I would like to thank my pastors in Sokoto, Dr. Moses Akor and Pastor Ben Musa for their prayers over my life. I am also grateful to my friend, Pastor Jonathan Oraka. Oraks, you have been a pillar of support. Thank you.

My deep gratitude goes to my RCN Lagos family, the first audience I taught the Field of Boaz message. Thank you for all your questions. I hope you find some answers here. The RCN Lagos pastors provided invaluable feedback that made my work easier, and they are a fantastic team.

I am immensely grateful to my publishing team, whose efforts have brought this book to life. I deeply appreciate Pastor Bridget Jangfa for working with me night and day in producing numerous drafts of this book and meticulously proofreading the final manuscript. I am grateful to Kemi Ugbegbua for her prompt and thorough editing of the
manuscript, despite the short notice.

Additionally, I express my gratitude to Pastor Jeremiah Mangut for his invaluable contributions to the research for this book. Special thanks go to my friend Olumide Adegoke for his creative genius in designing the cover. I commend Jonah Ikechukwu Dominic, my amazing publisher for his dedication and hard work.

I appreciate the encouragement of family and friends, especially those who kept asking, "when will your book be out?" It motivated me to complete this project. My wife and children are my greatest cheerleaders and deserve my thanks for their unwavering support. You are the best.

CONTENTS

CHAPTER THIRTEEN
MARRIAGE

<u>FOREWORD</u>

I do not prevaricate each time I get the opportunity to raise this alarm: the institution of marriage is under the most vicious attack from the darkest depths of hell!

The family, originally intended by God to be society's bedrock and building block, has been so sledge-hammered by social engineers and apostates almost to the point of handicap in the last few decades. I do believe that one of the apostolic responsibilities of the church of Jesus Christ at the close of this age is to raise the standards of heaven and wage a comprehensive war against the formations of hell at the home front until the tides of hell are pushed back and the Lordship of Jesus is established in the family.

At the turn of the century, we have seen some agents of darkness throw all caution to the wind and openly defy the order of God for marriage as flawlessly enshrined in the Bible. New man-concocted definitions and demonic programming, with their concomitant perversions, targeted at the institution of marriage are being radically propagated across all platforms in human civilisation today. The most unfortunate part is that these things have begun to find an inroad into the church. To the point that marriages in the church break down with divorce rates in the church almost eclipsing those in the world.

This work, The Field of Boaz, is a timely remedy for the ugly prevailing order in our day as it brilliantly intertwines the romance between Ruth and Boaz with the powerful testimony of my son, God's prophet, Austin J. Ukporhe. What strikes me the most is his courage to bring forth the story of his redemption in the most vulnerable yet powerful manner whilst gleaning heavily from the love affair of Ruth and Boaz. The message in this book is very clear: no mess is too big for God to clean and the believer can have the most fulfilling marriage no matter how atrocious their past was.

Indeed, Christian courtship and marriage are defined and regulated by the provisions of Scripture and the organic government of God that is brought to bear in the lives of believers as they continue in communion with the Holy Spirit. It is possible to run a courtship with the bed undefiled. There is a prescribed way to build a collapse-proof marriage under God. There is a sure way to climb above all worldly limitations and build a home that serves as heaven's tarmac on earth. Our faith is the victory that overcomes the world because it is not beholden to the world in principle and practice. All this and more have been powerfully captured by the author.

It is written in two parts and thirteen chapters, with Spirit-inspired action points at the end of each chapter to help the reader maximise God's wisdom and power contained within the volume of this tome, making it a very practicable read!

This work is a rich resource for the singles and married alike.
It is the byproduct of grace and mercy worked

through the vessel of the author, which is why I believe it will resonate with so many in the body of Christ; especially those with similar challenges that the Lord has helped the author to overcome. It is a solid testimony of things seen, heard, and handled in, by and through God which are both timely and timeless. I commend the author for a job well done and recommend this work to the body of Christ the world over.

Arome Osayi
Setman, Remnant Christian Network Global Makurdi, Benue State, Nigeria.

INTRODUCTION

Having been a pastor for over two decades now, I have had the privilege of speaking with many people on a wide range of topics. These conversations have covered interesting, inspiring, straightforward, critical, sometimes strange, and occasionally bizarre issues.

As I continued to interact with many young people, I grew increasingly concerned about some of the common proclivities I observed. As you know, many young people dream of getting married, but only a handful understand what it takes to make sound marital decisions. With this growing burden, I felt a leading to teach about marriage. But, I had doubts about my readiness. I needed direction. I also longed for something imbued with God's Spirit. So, I started seeking the Lord's face in prayer.

While I was praying and seeking guidance from the Lord, He instructed me to counsel singles and engaged couples in the church about marriage. This was the go-ahead that I had been anticipating. So, we began a teaching series titled "The Field of Boaz". The Field of Boaz started as a weekly Bible Study, where we explored God's word on the topics of singleness, marriage, and family life. Soon, we had filled the auditorium and sometimes had no space to accommodate the growing audience. After we had spent about ten weeks discussing the subject, I was confident that I had covered every aspect. I could not have been more mistaken. Many counselling sessions followed the teachings, and the questions came pouring in. I got all sorts of compelling questions, and it amazed me to discover the sheer number of people with genuine relationship problems. Calls kept flooding in, signifying that a few teachings and Q&A sessions were inadequate.

Some of the single men and women I spoke with believed they had made too many mistakes and, as a result, were unfit to find the right person in church. They were willing to accept whoever came their way. I also spoke with married people who voiced some troubling concerns. For some of them, marriage was a regretful mistake that they wished they could undo, while others were ready to leave and find happiness elsewhere. Some couples appeared to be going through the motions, lacking any genuine passion or excitement. To my surprise, these problems were described by tongue-speaking Christians who genuinely love the Lord and know His word.

I realise that many grey areas in relationships and marital issues exist because though the scriptures address these issues, to some people, they seem implicit or veiled. We must hold on to the wisdom of God and follow His guidance to understand them.

It is bewildering how many Christians are using the patterns and methods of the world yet expect to achieve a godly result. Unfortunately, we often look up to the wrong examples of courtship and marriage, some of which are even present within the church. The good news is that successful

Christian marriages exist in our time, and it is possible to have a successful marriage, regardless of your past or mistakes.

Part of the challenge is that many Christians are bent over by past weights, pulling them down and plunging them into depths of sorrow and feelings of unworthiness. The weight of past hurts, mistakes, and shame creates strongholds that keep many from receiving the Lord's blessings. Some Christians who have had a troubled past not only feel guilty but are also anxious about what lies ahead. Despite the assurance of God's grace and His works in their lives, the weight of their past is a great fear they struggle to shake off. Rather than trusting God's plan for their lives, they settle for less. Where do these self-imposed limitations and expectations come from? This book journeys through faith, hope, love, and redemption. Studying the romance of Ruth and Boaz and my redemption story, we see God's transformative power in turning pain into beauty. It illustrates grace for those who have strayed, guiding us to discover God's best on our journey to marriage, regardless of our past. It conveys the powerful message of Christ's redeeming grace and its accessibility to everyone who believes. Through my experiences as a man who has received mercy from the Lord, I share what I have learned. And if you desire to overcome past relationship mistakes, enter a Christian relationship, or lay the foundation for a loving and fulfilling marriage, this book is for you.

My greatest desire is for the Lord to heal wounded hearts and establish authentic relationships that will grow into successful marriages. I invite you to come along with me on this journey.

Ukporhe, A. J

SINGLE - INTENDED FOR GOOD

The desire for companionship is an innate part of the human nature. It is something we received from God Himself, and part of the expression of His love. God's intention for creating man was to allow for a relationship with Him. He wanted someone who could commune with Him. Therefore, He created man in His image and likeness:

And God said, "Let us make man
in our image, after our likeness"
(Gen 1:26)

We all crave companionship. God's intention for humanity is to live in companionship, not in isolation. He looked at all He had created and considered it good. Yet, something was amiss. He saw Adam alone with the animals and called the fact that he was alone "not good". In response to Adam's need for companionship, God formed Eve. And as soon as Adam beheld her, he knew without a doubt she would be his lifelong companion. He felt a sense of completion he had not experienced before. Thus he said:

This [is] now bone of my bones, and flesh of my flesh: she shall be called woman because she was taken out of Man. Therefore, shall A man leave his father and his mother, and shall cleave unto his wife: and they shall be one flesh. (Gen 2:23-24).

Our longing for intimacy is legitimate, spiritual, and scriptural. It is in God's perfect plan for us. This longing for friendship and fellowship is inherent in humanity, as designed by God.

Scientific research shows babies recognise friendship as an emotion before they even walk or talk. Some children create imaginary friends to practise new skills and to mimic real-life experiences. Here is a great example of this need for companionship. The 2000 movie Cast Away, stars Tom Hanks as protagonist Chuck Noland. Noland, a FedEx executive, became stranded on a deserted island after his plane crashed over the Pacific Ocean during a storm, leaving him the only survivor. Noland was stuck on the island for four years when his efforts to leave or contact help failed. In his desperate need to stay sane, he made a friend he named Wilson, a handmade volleyball. In the film, Wilson is Chuck Noland's anthropomorphic friend and his only companion for four years on the island. Wilson is reliable and mute, and although Wilson says nothing at all, he is a superb listener and a pleasant companion. His company made Chuck's life bearable amidst a hopeless situation. This allowed Chuck to have meaningful discussions, and even arguments, to preserve his sanity.

Wilson represents the need for companionship in our human existence.

In His omniscience, God saw the need for man to have companionship in fulfilling his divine purpose. Thus, he sculpted a woman who was his perfect match in every sense - this was the first marriage recorded in the Bible. Marriage is, without a doubt, a part of God's plan for humanity. It was

His idea for the man to fall in love with someone pleasing to Him and have marital intimacy. Therefore, to achieve the marriage God intended, one must know its author and His purpose, concepts, and principles. We may aver that the purpose of marriage is intertwined with God's divine purpose

for humankind, which is to exercise dominion over the earth. And while not everyone needs a spouse to fulfil their divine calling; for most people, like Adam, having a companion who shares God's vision is crucial to fulfilling His plan for them.

I have had extensive discussions with several couples experiencing difficulties in their marriages, and on the verge of breaking apart. Based on my investigations, I have concluded that the underlying causes of couples' issues in relationships or marriages are often fundamental, usually hinged on the foundational background of the individuals and the foundation on which they built the relationship. The early stage of a union, the initial meeting and courtship, are crucial in building a firm foundation. Indeed, many times, a myriad of other issues cause relationship problems, but as the Bible says,

If the foundations be destroyed,
what can the righteous do?
(Psa 11:3) NKJV

Because of this, it is essential to build relationships on the proper foundation. Relationships are built on the wrong foundation when people allow their experiences dictate their present actions. Unfortunately, many people dive into new relationships without taking the time to heal from past traumas or heartbreak. It does not matter what your history is or how dark your past appears; a successful marriage is possible if you let go of the past and embrace a new perspective on life. If you hold on to the details of your negative experiences, however, it will lead to problems in the future. But through faith, you can move beyond the negative aspects of your past and walk into God's plan and purposes for your future.

PART ONE

CHAPTER ONE

A BROKEN PAST

Surely I was sinful at birth, sinful from
the time my mother conceived me.
 (Psa 51:5) NIV

AUSTIN

People have referred to me by different names
throughout my life. These names were like markers
of time, each representing a different era and
embodying its unique essence. Eight days after I
was born in Tudun Wada, a small Muslim
community in Sokoto, North-West Nigeria, my
father gave me the name Okiotodoro. It means 'the
future is great' in my native Urhobo
dialect. My parents identified as Christians – in the

loose sense where in our environment, one was either Muslim or Christian, and they were not the former. So my mother named me Augustine-John. Augustine, meaning 'great, magnificent' and John, meaning 'God is gracious.' As a teenager - at the peak of my 'bad-boy' heydays, my friends nicknamed me Outlaw. My popular Hausa name was Bature, and, for the brief identity-seeking period when I experimented with Islam, I was Isah. The name Augustine-John will prove prescient of God's plans for my life and future; albeit one that I arrived at by the long way, through the hoops and hurdles the devil threw at me to prevent God's will. But before any of this, I was Austin.

AUSTIN

Seven years old and doing the things little boys do; playing with my friends during the year-round blistering Sokoto heat. The sweltering weather occasionally gave way to chilly early morning winds during the three-month harmattan season. I was the average little boy without a care in the world. And I had no hint of how my life would go skidding off the rails with a new entrant into our home.

AUNTY ANNA

Ah! Aunty Anna! She was my mother's cousin that came to live with us so she could have access to a better education. She was very close to my mom. Aunty Anna was gentle and kind, hardworking and ever-ready to help. She got us ready for school, helped with homework, and took care of us. Aunty even taught us how to speak Urhobo. She was an epitome of patience and well-mannered; my siblings and I liked her a lot. Aunty Anna did all the things aunties would do around the house. And she was the sweetest soul. She laughed and played with us. And she played with me. At first, it was funny whenever she would prod my ribs and stomach. She would tickle me and we would play. She laughed, and I laughed. She gradually advanced, and I would freeze whenever she did, but farther down, she would go. The entertainment became increasingly one-sided. Aunty would smile as I cringed, my heart hammering away like a tiny bird beating futile wings against my rib cage, as she softly encouraged me.

It was okay.

We were only playing.

But nobody played with me like this! Our innocent tickling turned into more intimate 'bed play.' Aunty would cuddle me in her bed and put my little body on top of hers. The first time I felt her warm, soft body under mine, my cerebrum struggled to process the deluge of feelings and emotions washing over me. It was an odd fusion of panic, dread, anticipation, exhilaration, and other sensations a seven-year-old boy had no business knowing. My heart raced, and my palms were slick with sweat. It looked like death was imminent. I was sure I would die. I was sure I should die. My heart was pounding so hard I thought it would burst out of my chest. It would have been better to die, even though I did not know what it entailed. My lower-middle-class parents were traditional in every sense of the word. Coming from a lineage of warriors, my grandfather, Ukporhe, made sure we were always secure. We had charms and incisions for everything - good luck, property protection, amulets to ward off sickness, and other totems to strengthen them. We had more charms to support the others – which needed to be renewed from time to time. I had incisions to protect me – long ones on my arm, left wrist, right wrist, and on my face. Ukporhe had a stellar reputation for providing top-notch protection. And we endured uncomfortably long trips on dusty roads from Sokoto to Ughelli in the South to reinforce our 'security.' After his death, my grandmother took over his role in 'securing my destiny'. One night, during one of those visits to my hometown, she laid me on a flat mattress that had the musky odour of a wet dog; on the top of my great-grandfather's grave while she threw white cowries on the ground and 'looked into my future'.

"Okiotodoro na strong man."
"Okiotodoro na better pesin born you."
"Okiotodoro na better pesin you be."

She said I would be a man of many men. I wish she had peered closer to home. She should have seen that they had inadvertently cooped the fox in with the hens. Because neither my grandfather and his protection — extensive as they were, nor my grandmother, with her seeing eyes, saved me from Aunty Anna.

Aunty Anna had firmly warned me never to tell anyone about our 'play play.' While I would never have dared mention it to my dad, my mother rewarded me for confiding in her with her open palm hotly landing on my thin face with a blinding swiftness that made me momentarily dizzy. She warned me
never to speak of such things. As you would expect, I never mentioned it to her again. Given the circumstances, I do not know if my mother ever confronted her. If she did, it made no difference. I learnt to manage my predicament as best as possible, keeping it to myself and never mentioning it to anyone else. I would squeeze my eyes shut and block out the world or my existence in the room as she moved my small body up and down hers. Sometimes, my imagination would run wild as I stared at a crack in the wall, picturing a narrow river there to transport me to distant lands. I could not help but wonder if the force of it was strong enough

to split the walls and bring the ceiling crashing down on us. And at other times, I was far away in my mind, chasing red-necked lizards with my friends, until she dampened her bedsheet with the streams of perspiration. Then she would return me to my bed or gently ask me to go. As the Chinese proverb wisely says, "To learn what is good, a thousand days are not sufficient; to learn what is evil, an hour is too long." By the time I was nine years old, I had become Anna's minor partner. During the holidays, when my father went out to work and my mom went to her shop, it was our time for mischief, to do 'play play.' Aunty Anna referred to our adventures as her drama, and soon invited other little girls from the neighbourhood. Despite my young age, I was still older than most of them. My friend's home became the perfect setting for our escapades, as it offered a convenient hideout. He lived with his mother, who sold Ice Water. Back then, women hawked water tied up in small polythene bags, which people bought to quench their thirst under the relentless Sokoto sun. Whenever his mother went out to fend for them, he provided us with a den for our heinous activities.

There was someone else; Anna's friend.

She was also a lead actress in our 'play, play'. The girls would undress as I would. As if things could not get any worse, my tiny phallus, already having a mind of its own, seemed to be more compliant than it should. When one persists in sin, it can mute their conscience, regardless of age. We were all young but deeply entangled in iniquity.

In John 8:34, **Jesus said, "I assure you: Everyone who sins is a slave of sin."** I was a slave to sin, a child slave. By the time I was in my teenage years, I was fully sexually active. Even after Anna returned to her hometown, I was sleeping around without care or remorse. By the time I became a young adult, I had several concurrent relationships with ladies and older women. My bad-boy lifestyle intensified, fuelled by a hostile and violent environment that offered the opportunity to become all sorts of things except good. A few Christians lived in the heart of this predominantly Muslim community. I was not a Muslim, and I was not what you would call a Christian, either. I knew little about

Christianity. And since all my friends were Muslims, I made multiple attempts to convert. They even gave me the name Isah. For some reason, however, I never made it to becoming a proper Muslim.

I wish I could say that my restlessness yielded positive outcomes, but it only caused me to spiral further out of control. I must admit that I persisted on this destructive path for quite some time. I was a rough boy in the actual
sense of the word. In my secondary school days, I frequented nightclubs that pulsed with blaring music and flashing lights. We would sneak out of the dormitory when it was dark and return just before sunrise. I remember some ladies would pass me a joint to smoke, but I never did. Despite having access to a steady supply of alcohol from my mother's trade, I did not drink. My sweet tooth prevented me from finding pleasure in something so sour, but I was a drug peddler. I sold marijuana. We called it 'wee-wee'. And I earned the nickname 'Outlaw' because I proved elusive. I was such a gangster. I found myself deeply entrenched in this gangster lifestyle, discreetly hiding my merchandise

and selling it to a diverse clientele. It included young and old, rich, poor, single, or married. I even sold my stash to law enforcement workers. All this was an augury of who I would become:

tough and independent. I was rugged. Sin and lawlessness had my life broken on many sides, fragmented beyond my ability to put the pieces back together, even if I wanted to. But the story gets interesting, for God is gracious.Have you lived a sinful life, or have you lived your life making only the wrong choices? You may have feelings of guilt, self-loathing, or a lack of self-worth because someone you trusted robbed you of your innocence. Perhaps you have been through things you cannot tell anyone else. Or your life may be spinning out of control, as mine was. We may choose to blame people, circumstances, and horrific experiences in these situations, but that will do nothing to change our situation. I have good news for you. It is not the end of the road, my friend; it is only the beginning of a journey. There is no situation too catastrophic for God to fix. A colourful life is still possible for you, and in the words of Shirley Hits, 'broken crayons still colour.'

RUTH

And they took them wives of the women of Moab; the name of the one was Orpah, and the name of the other Ruth: and they dwelled there about ten years. Mahlon and Chilion died, and the woman was left of her two sons and her husband. (Ruth 1:4) Ruth's story unfolds in the first chapter of the book of Ruth, starting with Elimelech, an Ephrathite living in Bethlehem,
Judah. Burdened by the relentless struggle to provide for his wife, Naomi and two sons, Mahlon and Chilion, Elimelech moved his family, against better judgement, from the famine ravished Bethlehem to Moab. They packed up their belongings and headed away from the land of promise, the land of blessing, through the rugged mountains and hills to the gentile land of Moab in an ironic pursuit of a better life.

***

As they journey through the arid land near the Dead Sea, the sun beats down with a blazing intensity that burns Naomi's crown and parches her throat. Shielding her eyes with her right palm, she squints into the distance, torn between hope and doubt, as she tries to catch a glimpse of what the future holds. She tightens her scarf, hoping to shield herself from the swirling dust that threatened to invade her nostrils, as she wonders at the dryness that had parched the earth beneath her blistering feet, its cracks spreading like giant spiderwebs. The oppressive weight of lifelessness hangs heavy in the air. It is permeated with the unmistakable smell of decay, an ominous sign of what is to come. The mark of the Lord's curse was evident in Moab, a pagan nation. Moab is tucked within the highlands of the Dead Sea in modern-day Jordan. The name Moab is derived from the peoples' lineage originating from Lot's incestuous affair with his daughters. Moab and his brother Ben-Ammi were born when Lot's two daughters, after losing their fiancés to the fires of Sodom and Gomorrah, slept with their intoxicated father to conceive children for themselves. And the firstborn said unto the younger, Our father is old, and there is not a man in the earth

to come in unto us after the manner of all the earth: Come, let us make our father drink wine, and we will lie with him, that we may preserve seed of our father. And they made their father drink wine that night: and the firstborn went in, and lay with her father; and he perceived not when she lay down, nor when she arose. And it came to pass on the morrow, that the firstborn said unto the younger, Behold, I lay yesternight with my father: let us make him drink wine this night also; and go thou in, and lie with him, that we may preserve seed of our father. And they made their father drink wine that night also: and the younger arose, and lay with him; and he perceived not when she lay down, nor when she arose. Thus were both the daughters of Lot with child by their father. And the first born bore a son, and called his name Moab: the same is the father of the Moabites unto this day. (Gen 19:31-37)

Elimelech made his home in Moab and soon died, leaving behind his wife and two sons. Meanwhile, Mahlon married a Moabitess - Ruth, and Chillon, his brother, married Orpah. After about a decade of dwelling in Moab, clearly unmost unfavourable conditions, both men also died. When we live outside the blessing of the Lord, it feels like everything starts to wither away, and we unknowingly step into the realm of the accursed. Life becomes a series of failures and losses, and we constantly face calamities when we walk out of the provisions and protection of God. I am convinced that was the case with Elimelech and his sons. The death of the three men meant a life of difficulty for their widows: Naomi, Ruth, and Orpah. They lost sustenance, confidence, and security. They lost the companionship and warmth of marriage. Losing Elimelech was difficult enough; Naomi also had to bear the torment of watching the world obliterated before the two young women she loved as her daughters. Ruth came from a culture with a tainted history — Moab, whom God had warned the Israelites to have nothing to do with. They were an accursed race. Moabites were enemies of God and the Israelites. As a result, Moabites were excluded from any association with Jewish communities. The Bible says, Follow me, for God has given your enemies—yes, Moab! —to you. (Judges 3:28) MSG

In Numbers 25, the men of Israel were led into sin by the women of Ruth's tribe. They were those with whom Israel 'began whoredom' and idolatry. Moabites were notorious for their sexual immorality, and their women led Israelite men astray. Moreso, Balak, the Moabite king, had paid Balaam to curse the children of Israel (Numbers 22-24). And it was because of Moab that twenty-four thousand people died in one day in the wilderness (Numbers 25:9-10). Ruth was tainted by the seemingly endless chronicles of negativity. In the preceding years, as captured in the third chapter of Judges, King Eglon of Moab, oppressed and enslaved Israel for eighteen years until they cried out to God to deliver them. The Lord raised Ehud from the clan of Benjamin, who drove his short, two-edged sword into Eglon's flabby stomach,

killing him. So, the children of Israel served Eglon the king of Moab eighteen years. But when the children of Israel cried unto the Lord, the Lord raised them up a deliverer, Ehud the son of Gera, a

Benjamite, a man left-handed: and by him the children of Israel sent a present unto Eglon the king of Moab. And Ehud put forth his left hand, and took the dagger from his right thigh, and thrust it into his belly. (Judges 3:14-15,21)

Like her people, Ruth, too, lived in idolatry. It was the life she had known from childhood. She grew up with the pagan worship of the dreadful Chemosh and Molech, and her people were described as the people of Chemosh. They were known for their exceptionally cruel practices, which involved sacrificing children and infants in the fiery flames as a tribute to their deity. Medieval French rabbi Schlomo Yitzchaki (Rashi), in his analysis of Jeremiah 7:31, described this form of worship and he says:

"...the high places of Topheth that is Molech, which was of copper, and they would heat it up from underneath it with its hands spread out and heated. And they would place the child on his hands, and he would be burnt and moan, and the priests would beat drums so that the father should not hear his son's voice and take pity. It is called Topheth because of the drum, Hinnom because of the child's moaning."

Ruth was raised in a heathen environment, surrounded by the worship of vile gods. Their thirst for blood was only rivalled by their appetite for the stench of the burning flesh of babies thrown into the flames beneath their mammoth stone images. Such practices were considered abominations in the eyes of the Lord, leading to His curse upon that land. Ruth, at that point in her life, was someone we would describe today as one who had not yet experienced redemption from the curse of the law. She was an unbeliever, unregenerated, and without salvation. As a heathen, she had no covenant with God and no claim to His inheritance. Her plight was indeed grim. Losing her husband left her feeling as though her entire universe had been obliterated. Whilst she grieved her loss, Ruth received the dreadful news that Naomi was departing for Bethlehem.

Naomi wanted to go home to her God. The famine had ended, and God had shown favour to His people. Having experienced so much anguish and bitterness, she considered herself to be Mara (Bitter), extremely grieved by the losses she had suffered in quick succession. It was this grief that moved her with the longing for her hometown. As Naomi prepared to leave for Judah, Ruth found herself at a crossroads, contemplating her options. She could choose to stay in Moab with her people, where she felt secure and familiar, or accompany her mother-in-law to a land she had only heard about. Naomi had been a source of strength and unwavering support to Ruth and Orpah. Their shared anguish during the difficult times had forged a deep bond between the three women.

Ruth discovered Yahweh from her husband's Hebrew family. She had glimpsed His loving nature in the lives of the Jewish household, yet never yielded to him. The decision before her was one that would shape her future and her relationship with God. Ruth found herself as an innocent victim of challenging circumstances, but the curse attached to her race was upon her. Idolatry arouses God's displeasure and wrath. It is a heinous affront to the tenets of monotheism. She had lived in direct disobedience to God by bowing to her gods. And while she remained under the terrible priesthood of Chemosh, she could not be free from misfortune. She was empty, pained, and broken. She suffered. However, she would soon make a life-changing detour, with eternal consequences.

Indeed, hard-hitting challenges sometimes compel us to make wiser decisions and take action. Life may have thrown terrible experiences our way, such as dealing with abuse, battling a terminal illness, coping with the loss of a loved one, or struggling with a sinful past. In the face of such trials, we are left with choices: to wallow in our pain, cling to guilt and remain trapped, or to gather our bags release the burden, and embark on a path of deliverance and healing. Your situation might be similar to mine or Ruth's, where you have lived a life devoted to serving lusts or bowing to other gods. Do not lose heart. A clearer path lies ahead.

Grace is readily available, and when accepted, it has the power to transform your weak and sandy foundation into a firm one— anchored on Christ, the solid rock. The destination you reach depends on the choices you are willing to make from this point onward. By surrendering to the Lordship of Jesus and allowing Him to take absolute control of our lives, we can make significant progress and move towards a more fulfilling and purposeful path.

PRAYER

I pray for anyone reading this who has experienced or is currently dealing with any form of sexual abuse or other sinful bondage. In the name of Jesus, I bind up your broken heart. I break the chains of lies and deception that have held you captive. I release you into the truth of who you are in Christ. I proclaim liberty to every captive, and the opening of the prison to anyone who is bound in Jesus' name. Amen.

ACTION POINTS

1. Take some time for self-reflection and introspection.

2. Are there experiences from your childhood that you need

to address for personal growth and healing?

CHAPTER TWO

LETTING GO

Forget the former things; do not dwell on the
past. See, I am doing a new thing!
(Isaiah 43:18) NIV

AUSTIN

My decision to change my old lifestyle came from
an encounter at the height of my recklessness. My
parents' financial status improved significantly, so
we moved from Tudun Wada, where I engaged in a
life of independence, lawlessness, and hostility, to
Old Airport, which was predominantly Christian.
That was the best decision my parents ever made
because it was the start of a consciousness of
Christianity and what it entailed. Before that time,
we only identified as Christians because we were
not Muslims. We considered ourselves Christians,
but we also observed several pagan practices. My

family started going to church occasionally because there was one close by. I made some friends in our new church,

although we stuck to the back and were the backbenchers. I still visited Tudun Wada regularly because I had an existing clientele I needed to keep up with. Also, my guys and girlfriends were still there. Everything appeared to be going well until my sins caught up with me.

On a cold Thursday night - a rarity in Sokoto - a searing pain on my back, waist, and arms awakened me. I tried pulling my blanket over me, but someone yanked it off my body, and the sharp pain continued jabbing at me. My Dad was flogging me with his koboko as he hurled insults at me until I jumped out of bed. This was not the first time I had been awoken like this. Looking back, I wonder how I did not go mad. But that night, it was different. My father was seething with rage. As I leapt to my feet, wide awake, he grabbed me by my trousers and dragged me into our dimly lit living room. This was around midnight! I was trying to figure out what I had done wrong this time as I struggled to put on my bathroom slippers. As we got to the parlour, I instantly knew what the problem was. Seated on our brown cushion, with her head down, was Beatrice, my girlfriend, along with her parents and cousin. With my parents, they formed the quorum that was to decide my fate that midnight. My Dad was still holding on to the waist of my trousers as though I was a thief, and I knew I would have to escape or die there. Without wasting a moment, and to their consternation, I flung off his hand and, with one hand holding onto my beltless trousers, darted through the back door to the backyard. I jumped over the fence into the dark. My father's voice echoed behind me in the still night. Amidst profanities, he howled...

"Make sure you never come back to my house! You're not my son!"
"Be going!"
"You can go, since me and you cannot stay under the same roof."
"You're not my ..."

Those words, carriers of my father's outrage, reverberated with my heartbeat. Something inside me went cold that night. I knew he was serious. My Dad was always serious. And even though we did not have such an excellent relationship, I still preferred what we had to the thought of being rejected outright. He said he was no longer my father, seeing that he had done all he could to help me change and stop sleeping with 'people's daughters'.

"You're not my son!"

Those words that splattered out of his mouth morphed into creatures that roamed around in my thoughts as I walked to my friend's house at the far end of the street. The place that would be my new home for the next couple of months. The passage of time would eventually prove that my father meant every word he said that night. At this point in my life, I felt like I was being sucked into a vacuum. Here I was, nineteen years old, expecting a child that I was neither ready to father nor own. The sting of my father's rejection was painful, but what made it even harder to bear was the agreement from my typically supportive mother. Yet, my mind, buoyed by youthful exuberance, convinced me that perhaps this was a good thing- a pure stroke of luck. I was a man now, and I needed my space, after all.

Every once again, I would walk down the road, greet my mom at the gate; and collect stuff – shirts, trousers, shoes and a Walkman from my younger brother. Frankly, the boy in me wanted to go back home and beg my parents. I wanted to hear something else, to have things turn out differently. My mind, like an active volcano, was flooded with many thoughts. I was free to run my life, but when would my parents let me return home? I thought about my sisters. And I thought about Beatrice; how had she let her family find out that she was pregnant? I wondered how things had spiralled out of control.

Beatrice's parents were insistent that we "do something" about the situation. They did not want a stain on the family name, so I played my role and funded the project. When I saw her a few weeks later, and asked about it, she responded in a mumbled, shaky voice.

I changed the topic. It is hard to forget the unease that crawled down my spine that day. Despite all this, I continued my reckless lifestyle until I had a life-altering experience that completely transformed me.

TURNING POINT

On September 14th, 1999, I hopped on a motorcycle, heading to Tudun Wada to meet the guys as usual. But that day, the feeling of emptiness that had been haunting me returned with a vengeance. The weight of it was so heavy, and my heart seemed to skip random beats. As the wind brushed against my face, I sensed something more than just a breeze. It was like this force wrapped around me like a warm, thick blanket - so powerful, yet so gentle. Heat like a ball of fire burned in the pit of my stomach. Its fingers were all over my skin till I was flushed with sweat. Then I heard these words, resonating from somewhere like a well; deep, and distant, yet as an echo from within me

"Why do you want to live your life like this?"
"Do you want to self-destruct?"
"Give me your life, and I will turn it around."

Tears cascaded down my cheeks relentlessly. I wanted to return home, or rather, to the place I called home. It felt like I was burning with a fever, so perhaps lying down would help. I needed to find a quiet place, but had no willpower to tell the motorcycle rider to make a U-turn. The halting of the bike broke into my thoughts. Frantically wiping my face, I pulled out some naira notes from the back pocket of my baggy denim shorts and paid my fare. As I made my way to the room, the vibration of loud, familiar music pulsed towards me. My friends were all present: Dojja, Rambo, Garba, Abubakar, Pius, along with their girlfriends. I could barely speak as I walked in, shaken as I was from my motorcycle experience. Something had happened to me; I knew I might have encountered God. Still jolted and quiet, I stood in the middle of the room as my eyes adjusted to the dimness in our hangout, poorly lit with green bulbs and oozing with the smell of cigarettes, marijuana, alcohol, and cheap local perfume. Seeing that I was reticent and calm, they tried to pull me out of my 'mood' by hailing me.

"Outlaw is around."

There was a mattress on the floor. Maintaining a straight face, I sat on it and rested my back on the wall.

Outlaw.

For some reason, hearing that name which had been my nickname - my badge of pride for many years - infuriated me. I no longer wanted to be called 'Outlaw'. It had suddenly become anathema.

"You guys should leave me alone," I mumbled with a frown. *"My name is Austin." "You guys should just call me Austin."*

They collapsed with laughter while I held my frown. They responded with handshakes and more praise. They were mocking and guffawing.

"What?" Dojja looked at me with suspicion. "He is high," he said.

More laughter.

The room quickly turned into a boisterous symphony of laughter, chatter, and music-making. Under different circumstances, I would be right in the middle of it, freestyling - everyone around knew me for 'spitting bars' in the clubs. But not today. It was different today, and I was not myself. A myriad of inexplicable thoughts and feelings tumbled over themselves inside me. And there was a fire within me, with an intense energy that seemed to explode from the depths of my being. Indeed, God was at work. Now I knew without question it had to be Him. I felt an urgent need to leave. We had planned to fool around that day. It was the reason we assembled in that dingy room that I rented with earnings from my marijuana sales.

But God is merciful. He came for me that day.

He was on my case, and in His infinite mercy, He kept my girlfriend, Hauwa, from coming. If she had been there, she would have helped me out of my 'mood'. My heart thumped louder than a bass drum, and I wiped my sweaty palms on the back of my shorts again and again. After a short while, I strode out of the room in search of the voice that had spoken to me.

The motorcycle ride to Celebration Chapel occurred at jet speed. I had no idea that my life was about to take a new turn just as speedily. Before long, we were at the church building. The bike came to a stop. I paid my fare with a crumpled, worn-out note and walked into the wide-open entrance of the auditorium as if walking into the embrace of a waiting saviour. Regret had also quietly crept in with me, and sat deep within my stomach, doing its job. And as I ambled on the aisle, pew after pew, my heart sank with sorrow. I crouched at the altar,

shaky but with a renewed sense of awe for the God I
had disregarded for so long. From the depths of my heart, I whispered a plea, asking Him to forgive my sins and help me change. That was all I remember saying; and the moment I uttered those words, a powerful force I now know to be the Holy Spirit came upon me, and I started babbling words. Mumbling at first, then I was blurting and bellowing indecipherable words. Faster, and much faster. I was speaking in tongues – the very thing my friends and I had mocked church people for doing. I was quivering. A ball of fire roared within me, desperate to burst out with those unfamiliar words. I was no longer whispering, now I was shouting, kicking, hitting benches, falling, clutching my stomach, and rolling on the floor with violent power. The more I tried to compose myself, the more I failed. I stood up, but it only made things worse. Everything was happening simultaneously.

Those around must have sent for the Pastor. When he came infrom his office, as I lay panting on the concrete floor, he said,

"It is his time; I have been praying for him."

Jesus, in John 6:44 says: **"No man can come to me, except the Father which hath sent me draws him."**

No one comes to Jesus on their own. It starts with an invitation, a divine drawing by God the Father within that person's heart. God lifts the veil that blinds their minds from seeing the light of the glorious gospel of Christ (2 Corinthians 4:4).

And He often does this riding upon the intercession of the saints. Before a person is saved, there would be someone somewhere raising intercession on their behalf. This was my experience. The Father drew me to Jesus, and the pastor's prayers, along with those of others whose names I will never know, made this possible. For this, I am eternally grateful.

RUTH
And Ruth said, intreat me not to leave thee, or to return from following after thee: for whither thou goest, I will go; and where thou lodgest, I will lodge:

thy people shall be my people, and thy God my God: Where thou diest, will I die, and there will I be buried: the LORD do so to me, and more also, if ought but death part thee and me. When she saw that she was steadfastly minded to go with her, then she left speaking unto her. (Ruth 1:16-18)

The three women begin their journey towards Bethlehem. Naomi's steps resound with the hope of returning home. But the path ahead grows steep with doubt, and soon, like a shadow cast upon her aspirations, a gnawing uncertainty takes root. Turning to her daughters trudging behind her, she urges them to reconsider, to turn back. Yet they refuse to be dissuaded, for, over the years, they have shared a strong bond with their mother-in-law. Like a tapestry, this bond was a beautiful and intricate pattern of shared moments, joyful and sorrowful.

The wind whispers tales of uncertainty, and the journey ahead a tangle of hope and hesitation, a poignant tableau of choices made and the unspoken sacrifices that lie ahead. Indeed, Naomi knows that the life of an unmarried foreign widow in those climes is difficult without the comfort and safety of

family and the familiar. She knows this first-hand. She has lived this life in Moab. And it is not a life that she wants for her daughters. Bethlehem may not be the best place for widowed Moabitesses to start over. She presses on them to return. Perhaps as a necessary discouragement or a test to see if their hearts are genuinely drawn to Yahweh. But the young women love Naomi too much to stay behind.

"Go back"

"What?" They react in shock.

"Go back home. You cannot come with me." "Go back. Moab is your home. Bethlehem is too far away, and you have no one there,

go…"

"But we have you." Ruth interrupts.

"You are our family."

But the older woman is determined. *"We buried your husbands in Moab. And I have no more sons who will marry you. Please. Go back."*

Orpah says through sobs, *"We will go with you, mother..."* Naomi walks away with determination, wiping her tears with her veil.

"You have shown me kindness; I will remember you with warmth and tenderness. May the God of Israel show you the..."

"We will never leave you," Ruth interrupts, determined.

"I will go with you."

"Return to Moab."

"Many good men there will sell what they have to have the warmth
of your love..."

"Return."

With a warm kiss and tear-filled eyes, Orpah reluctantly turns to leave. Naomi turns to Ruth, fixated on the spot; she blesses her while trying to persuade her.

"See, your sister is leaving to be with your people, to serve your gods. She hasn't gone far. Go with her, my daughter. May the Lord bless and keep you and return the kindness you have shown even to the dead. May you find peace and goodwill."

"Don't force me to leave, Mother." She wails. Ruth clasps her mother-in-law's hand as if her life depended on it. *"I will follow you to Bethlehem."*

But Naomi is thinking to herself, Surely, this young woman knows nothing about Bethlehem. A

Moabitess may not be welcome there.

"Ruth...You... I...listen to me, there is no place there for..."
But Ruth is adamant.

"Mother, where you go, I will go. Where you live, I will live. Your people will be my people. Your God will be my God. I will be with you, and only death will separate me from you."

***

Orpah kissed Naomi farewell and left, but Ruth cleaved. Does it remind yo of Judas who kissed, and of John who cleaved? Judas betrayed Jesus with a kiss, and Orpah separated from Naomi (and the possibility of a glorious future). She made the seemingly logical decision to leave the unknown and return to the familiar. She went back into her life of idolatry, separated from the true God. Ruth, who had truly let go, progressed into God's redemptive plan. She insisted on leaving everything behind and followed Naomi to serve the God of the Jews. How many times do we see people act like Orpah? Initially committed to following Jesus, they revert to sinful ways when they realise the uncertainty of the future. For Ruth, it was not so. She set her face like a flint - pushing forward. This brings to mind a story of soldiers during a war. Whenever they disembarked from their ships and the battle grew intense, they would retreat into their vessels and sail away. The generals overseeing them grew increasingly dissatisfied with this recurring pattern and sought a new commander to address the issue. The commander waited until every soldier was ashore, then set the vessel ablaze. With the battle raging, the soldiers had to hold their position and fight since they were trapped between the ocean and the enemy's increasing power. Their resilience allowed them to push through the opposition until they emerged victorious. This was Ruth's mind-set. She burnt her ships behind her and any bridge that connected her to her past, and she forged ahead into a new life. Despite being married to Jewish men, scripture refers to the women as 'Moabitesses' and it is unknown if they followed the

Jewish faith. Had Ruth been converted when she married Mahlon, perhaps there would be no allusion to Naomi urging her to return to her people and gods as she concluded upon Orpah's leaving. Did they accept Judaism from a sincere desire to be part of the Jewish nation, or was it for love and the desire to please their husbands?

Verse 15 says, "Look," said Naomi, "your sister-in-law is going back to her people and her gods. Go back with her." (Ruth 1:15) NIV.

Have you ever felt alone in your life? Or have you felt like you hit rock bottom? That was precisely how Naomi felt as she left Moab like a prodigal daughter returning home. So, when we find ourselves in unfortunate situations, and it seems our past is in the way, we need to let go to enjoy the beauty of the future entirely. Holding onto the past does not just put limitations on us; it demands our energy and focus. Letting go allows us to live within the possibility of discovering and living in God's perfect will for us. Regardless of where you have been, with whom you have been, or what you have done, there is always a new day and plenty of opportunities for a fresh start.

Too often, we allow regret, guilt, and pain, keep us down. Sure, no one has a perfect past, but drowning in self-pity and remorse would not steer you right either. Instead, they become roadblocks on your journey forward. The decisions you make shape the course of your life. The only way to progress is to move forward because a flawed past cannot sustain you. Do not stay in the dust any longer. Pick up where you left off and move forward.

Let me share with you a story I read of three men written by Norman Wright in his inspiring book entitled *The Perfect Catch*. He writes,

'Once upon a time, there were three men. Each man had two sacks, one tied in front of his neck and the other tied on his back. When the first man was asked what was in his sacks, he said, "In the sack on my back are all the good things friends and family have done. That way they're hidden from view. In the front sack are all the bad things that have happened to me. Every now and then I stop, open the front sack, take the things out, examine them, and think about them." Because he stopped so much to concentrate on all the bad stuff, he really did not make much progress in life. The second man was asked about his sacks. He replied, "In the front sack are all the good things I've done. I like to see them, so quite often I take them out to show them off to people. The sack in the back? I keep all my mistakes in there and carry them all the time. Sure, they're heavy. They slow me down, but you know, for some reason I can't put them down." When the third man was asked about his sacks, he answered, "The sack in front is great. There I keep all the positive thoughts I have about people, all the blessings I've experienced, all the great things other people have done for me. The weight isn't a problem. The sack is like sails of a ship. It keeps me going forward."The sack on my back is empty. There's nothing in it. I cut a big hole in its bottom. In there I put all the bad things that I can think about myself or hear about others. They go in one end and out the other, so I'm not carrying around any extra weight at all.'

Ruth's conversion happened when she left everything behind and followed Naomi wholeheartedly, placing her faith in a God who would never leave nor forsake her. She would not go back to her old lifestyle of idol worship.

She cut a hole in the baggage of yesterday, walked the path of wisdom, and saw through the lens of faith, changing her life forever.Ruth was saying: *I am ready to make a change.* Here, a Moabitess, a stranger, deciding to follow her mother-in-law to serve a new and unknown God, leaving her father's house, to a land she did not know. Does this not remind you of Abram? Let me give you some context as to the gravity of this situation.

In those days of pagan polytheism, a person's gods were intimately and intricately woven into the fabric of their heritage, family, and culture. It was difficult to abandon your gods. Ruth's decision to turn away from her gods was not just a mere walk in the park; or out of it. That defining moment, when she turned aside, she was leaving behind everything that was once her life. Unlike Orpah, who retraced her path to her people, her gods and her former way of life, Ruth put one foot forward, leaving her past behind completely. She stepped into krher future.

You might be asking yourself, what about me? I have also been through a lot in life. God's word says, Therefore, if any man be in Christ, he is a new creature: old things are passed away; behold, all things are become new.
(2 Corinthians 5:17)

If you have not yet made the decision to give your heart to Jesus and accept Him as your Saviour and Lord, then that is the initial and most significant step to take on this journey.
Please pray this prayer with me:

Heavenly Father, I come to you knowing that You are merciful, kind and abounding in love to all who call on you. I believe Jesus died to save all sinners, and I now surrender to His authority over my life. I

acknowledge I am a sinner and have lived outside your authority. Please forgive me for all my sins. Please give me a new life and fill me with your Holy Spirit. In Jesus' name. Now it is time to seek the leadership of the church to guide
you on this fresh path of life. I want you to exercise your faith by believing that you are a beloved child of your Heavenly Father. He loves you with an unconditional love. He will cleanse you. And now He says to you, live! Receive your acceptance in God today, and you will live again.

Sister, live!
Brother, live!

RENEW YOUR MIND
What do you see?
Are you fixating on the failures of yesterday?
What do you call yourself?
Do you consider yourself a worthless object?
Do you feel guilt and shame? Do you feel alone and desolate?

My brother, my sister, you will never change the direction of your life until you change the focus of your sight. What you see in your mind, you will have in time. It is time to see yourself through the lens of God's word. God's forgiveness is complete if you genuinely seek it. He does not judge us based on our history; neither does He keep a record of our wrongs. With genuine repentance, He wipes our sins away and gives us a new beginning. You should forgive yourself, just as He has. See yourself as forgiven and set yourself free from the bondage of self-pity. I tell you, holding on to our wrongs is not a sign of humility but evidence that we have not entirely accepted the redemptive power of God and its benefits. Therefore, 'come out of your father's house', and let go of every guilt, shame and pain. Jesus does not hold on to them. Neither should you.

Arise. Make a fresh start. You have a place in God, and He wants to birth something that will echo through eternity through you. God can use your ashes for His glory.

The prospect of starting over is daunting, but you can pause at any point in your life and hit the reset button. Unlike Ruth, who made a pivotal decision in her critical moment, to forsake her gods and serve the living God, in my case, God pursued me through His sovereign will. When God comes for us or we yield ourselves to Him, He takes us through the process of sanctification and renewal. He will not turn a blind eye to your weaknesses; rather, He will work on them one by one, transforming you into the person He intends you to be.

I recently came across a journal that got my attention. Its front cover features this powerful quote attributed to the ancient philosopher, Socrates. My intention is to underscore the message. It says:

"The secret of change is to focus all of your energy not on fighting the old, but on building the new."

That was precisely what I did, thanks to the guidance of my pastor and new mentor. Following the encounter I had in the church, I gathered my belongings, which were minimal this time, and moved from Kelvin's house to the church. I packed light, only bringing a few clothes and a notebook. I did not even own a Bible. Like the young woman Ruth, I left everything else behind, as though they were paraphernalia connecting me to my vagabond past. I had moved out of my parents' home only a few months earlier. Disowned and fatherless, I was free to do as I pleased, but it had turned out to be pyrrhic freedom. So, here I was, leaving this freedom, and living in the strangest of places – a church, because I had found one on whom I could depend – God.

Of all personalities, God.

I was not sure whom I believed was my new father, God Himself or the church – my community of pastors and brethren. But one thing was certain: I had found a new family – God's family.

Experiencing the weight of God's mercy transforms a person. The sinful acts that were once so appealing and vital to their existence become lacklustre and drab. Sin becomes repugnant as this person uncovers a more profound life and inheritance in the kingdom of God. Life took a different turn for me, and I found a new definition and meaning to it. I discovered that only Jesus could give me a meaningful life. So, I resolved to hold on to Him, and never let go.

Ezekiel 16:6 says,
And when I passed by thee, and saw thee polluted in thine own blood, I said unto thee when thou wast in thy blood, Live; yea, I said unto thee when thou wast in thy blood, Live.

As I mentioned earlier, it is crucial to let go of the past. Living in the past involves fixating on our mistakes and missed opportunities, constantly ruminating over the choices we should or should not have made, and dwelling on things we did or failed to do. Instead of embracing the present and looking toward the future, we find ourselves trapped in a cycle of regret over what might have been. Living in the past also means holding onto the memories of people we have lost and the opportunities that slipped away. This sense of longing and regret can become overwhelming. It involves harbouring resentment and assigning blame to others or circumstances for our current situation. Holding onto fragments of what was once whole, coupled with regret and a feeling of confinement, only serves to hinder our progress.

When we attempt to move forward while clinging to the past, it is like cycling uphill and looking downhill. Or driving with one foot on the accelerator and the other on the brake. This dual effort, though arduous, proves to be both counterproductive and irrational.

I remember when I was still learning to drive. While on the center lane of the freeway, I would be overly conscious of the vehicles speeding up behind me on the left route, and, more often than not, I focused on the rear-view mirror, instead of looking ahead, diverting my attention from the road. This constant backward glance was a recipe for disaster, as it pulled me from the momentum I should have been building. My looking back slowed me down where I needed to speed, while my squatting on the fast lane slowed everyone else behind me. This situation created an unintended paradox: an open freeway stretched ahead, while a tailback of needless traffic formed behind. My problem created problems for the drivers behind me. It is simple: you cannot move forward while looking backwards, and you are a drag on the people looking up to you. Little wonder cars have large windscreens and small rear-view mirrors. Our focus should be in front, not behind.

It is time to look ahead, forget those things that are behind and press on to what is ahead of you. Have faith and believe. The strength of your faith is tested when you face the highest mountains.

PRAYER

Lord Jesus, I confess all my sins. Forgive me and cleanse me from all unrighteousness. Show me your mercy and your kindness, and help me let go of any way of life that does not please you. Please help me forget all the former things and give me a new heart in Jesus' name.

ACTION POINTS

1. Let Go of the Past: Just as Ruth left her old life behind, release the baggage of your past to embrace a new beginning in Christ.

2. Embrace Change: Change is not always easy, but it is worth it.

3. Focus on the Present and the Future: Keep your eyes on what lies ahead rather than being caught up in past regrets.

4. Accept God's forgiveness.

5. Build a Strong Support System: You need the support
of godly people around you to help in times of change and difficulty.

CHAPTER THREE

A NEW LIFESTYLE

Here is a trustworthy saying that deserves full

acceptance: Christ Jesus came into the world

to save sinners—of whom I am the worst. But

for that very reason, I was shown mercy so that

in me, the worst of sinners, Christ Jesus might

display his immense patience as an example for

those who would believe in him and receive

eternal life. (1 Tim 1:15-16) NIV

AUSTIN

For the second time within several months, I was homeless again, albeit voluntarily. Evicted from home, I had now left my arrangement with Kelvin following my encounter with the Lord. I was sleeping on a church bench. I slept there for so long that this 'Outlaw' became a 'praying mantis' and Celebration Chapel (now called Christ House) became my permanent address. This is a scenario I would never have imagined - living there for the next two years. During my early days of being born again, the brethren introduced me to a life of communing with God. This was the threshing floor stage of my life. I went through a season of intense prayer, fasting and genuine consecration under the firm guidance of the Pastor, Rev. Moses Akor. This once recalcitrant young man had found a new mentor. 'Pastor' introduced me to intercession, and we prayed along with the other brethren who also lived in the church storeroom. For the first eight months of my living in church, I joined them for long hours of prayers. We would pray in tongues non-stop for long stretches - morning, noon, and night. For someone unfamiliar with this reality, it felt surreal. Sometimes we went on extended periods of fasting. In no time, the news of my conversion and transformation spread. My old friends, who thought I would backtrack, had to acknowledge that something extraordinary had happened to me. In my newfound community, my hunger for God deepened and intensified. I had a voracious desire to explore and to know God. During the purge, I learnt many things. I learnt to speak responsibly, dress appropriately, and become a proper man. Oh! God bless the young men whose clothes I wore until I could purchase mine. In those days, certain clothing styles were associated only with rebels, and that was mostly what I had.

I learnt to love. I learnt brotherhood; true brotherhood, poles apart from what I used to know. We shared what we had, and if anyone had, everyone had. We connected on a level deeper than anything I had experienced before. It was as if I had known them from another life. I had found my spiritual tribesmen.

I was letting go, loosening myself from the strings that held me to the past. The pastors groomed and drilled me in much fasting and prayer, and my growth was evident. I witnessed the supernatural dimensions of God as I prayed for sick people, and they recovered. My heart was open to learning new things, and I was as eager as I was expectant. This was fuel to the fire that burned within me. During that period, I buried my head in my Bible. I accompanied Pastor Moses to many preaching events and crusades. I still believe the Lord gave me such accelerated growth because I had gone too far down the wrong path and was running out of time. My journey on the path of life had begun. And I had a lot of ground to cover.

Two key elements necessary to achieve success are teachability and tenacity. And as much as this was a time of growth and tangible encounters with the Lord, I have to admit; it also proved to be a time of difficulty in many shades. Because I was no longer the kingpin I used to be, I had no choice but to depend on the generosity of the church leadership that catered to our welfare.

The church was consistently meeting our needs, for which I am eternally grateful. Yet sometimes, the weight of my financial strain was difficult to bear. By God's mercies, I never once thought about reaching out to my old friends or family for support, even when things were difficult. I knew it was not the right thing to do. I was going through a season of dealings under the Holy Spirit, so I had to remain submitted to him. This is pivotal because not every season of lack is a dealing from the Holy Spirit. Sometimes such a season could result from sheer carelessness, laziness, or misinterpretation of our signs and promptings. Discernment is crucial. A pure desire for God will help purify your heart so you can discern and follow the Spirit's prompting. Another experience I had was that my encounters with God's Spirit seemed to have abruptly stopped coming. I could no longer sense His tangible presence on my body, and around me like in the early days of my being born again. It was reasonably alarming to me, as I felt God had abandoned me. It felt like He had led me into a trap, only to vanish when I had fully committed; and I know many Christians experience this. After accepting the calling deep within your spirit and coming to God, there may be a season where He waits for you to seek Him. Jeremiah 29:11-13 captures this.

For I know the thoughts that I think toward you, says the Lord, thoughts of peace and not of evil, to give you a future and a hope. Then you will call upon Me and go and pray to Me, and I will listen to you. And you will seek Me and find Me, when you search for Me with all your heart.

It starts with God telling us He has good and peaceful thoughts, which is His will and desire for our lives. However, he does not fully reveal these thoughts to us. So, we need to pray to Him, believing He will unveil His will to us. Then He makes us understand that the only way we can find His will is when we find Him first, and the only way we can find Him is when we seek Him with 'all' our hearts, not a fraction.

Seeking God is a sign that we love Him and have faith in Him. God desires to be found by us, but only after we have searched for Him with all our hearts, and He reveals Himself in ways that are beyond our understanding. Learning this protocol early kept me going during those difficult times.

During challenging times, we feel like we are backed into a corner with no way out. These times of testing serve as a measure of the strength of our faith. Faith was my anchor. I had come to know and believe too much in God's love to turn away. Jesus' teaching in John 6 rattled the disciples such that many left because the way of the kingdom appeared too difficult. So, He asked His twelve disciples if they would go also.

See their response:
Peter replied, "Master, to whom would we go? You have the words of real life, eternal life. We're already committed ourselves, confident that you are the Holy One of God." (John 6:68-69)

I experienced this life and would not renege on my promise. I hung on to God. I had burned the bridges behind me.

So, Naomi returned, and Ruth the Moabitess, her daughter in law, with her, which returned out of the country of Moab: and they came to Bethlehem at the beginning of barley harvest. (Ruth 1:22)

Like prodigals returning to their God, the two women arrive Judah, barely able to put one foot in front of the other. Naomi had taken the long road home. Literally. As memories flooded back, her nostalgia grew to a crescendo and tears welled up in her eyes. The scent of barley, the throng of traders buying and selling along the dusty road, and the chatter of people everywhere signalled the ongoing harvest. Harvest time in Judah is busy both day and night. Naomi had told Ruth about this, but she did not quite imagine it would be as boisterous. Ruth looks around, taking in the orderly disorderliness of the place. At first, no one pays them any attention, except for a handful of stares. Then one woman, an elderly one, with eyes and mouth wide open, a blend of shock and recognition on her pale face, screams.

"Is that Naomi?"

"Naomi?"

"Naomi!"

"Does Naomi also have a daughter?"

"Where is Elimelech?"

"Naomi!"

The crowd is stirred because of them, and everyone speaks simultaneously. Ruth, because of Naomi, suddenly found herself enfolded in the bosom of women she had not met before. She was engulfed in the warmth of strangers, women who would become part of her new life. The sun is already setting in Bethlehem, as it is over Ruth's past. Her new life has just begun.

***

Letting go and leaving our past behind is a significant step towards progress. But that is only the beginning. Letting go is just the first step. What is equally important is making the necessary changes in our lifestyle to adapt to our new reality. new way of living is a clear indication of the transformation that has occurred within us. It is the evidence that we have encountered the Great One and have been changed from within. When Ruth accompanied Naomi on this path of life, she purposed to adopt new traditions and practices. She was in a foreign civilisation where she looked different, dressed different, talked different, and had to learn to do things differently.

While yearning for acceptance among the Israelites, Ruth had to adopt a new culture opposed to hers. Yet she remained, continuing among a people, some of whom believed women like her were only good at leading Israelite men into worshipping idols. (Numbers 25:1-5 and 1Kings 11:1-8).

Like a sore thumb, she stood out, but with Naomi's loving guidance and protection, the grace she found led her, guided her and schooled her. Ruth had to observe the Shabbat, beyond her experience, while her husband was alive. She partook in the elaborately celebrated Rosh Hashanah. She fasted and prayed to God at the time of Yom Kippur, her new friends and sisters guiding her in this way of life. She may have felt out of place with the many stares she received, yet she forged ahead. Not long afterwards, she blended in with God's people. We are no different from Ruth. When we turn a new leaf, we may feel out of place and have to learn and unlearn certain things. To fully embrace our new life in Christ, we must always not all alter our dress sense as I did, but beyond that make a conscious effort to break old habits and walk in a way that aligns with our beliefs. What we need in such moments is to have faith and patience.

By her declaration to follow Naomi and accept her God and her people, Ruth:

1. Obtained Salvation
She denounced her gods, left her family, and her old ways. Becoming saved and accepted in the commonwealth of God's people, she was brought into the economy of God. Ruth came into the life that stems from God, a life which transcends death.

2. Embraced Sanctification
She separated herself from the 'old man' – putting

off her former conduct, becoming renewed in the spirit of her mind by integrating into her new spiritual environment. In the book of Ephesians, the writer skilfully captures this reality:

But that's no life for you. You learned Christ! My assumption is that you have paid careful attention to him, been well instructed in the truth precisely as we have it in Jesus. Since, then, we do not have the excuse of ignorance, everything—and I do mean everything—connected with that
old way of life has to go. It's rotten through and through. Get rid of it! And then take on an entirely new way of life—a God-fashioned life, a life renewed from the inside and working itself into your conduct as God accurately reproduces his character in you. (Ephesians 4:20-24) MSG

3. Acquired an Inheritance
She came into the inheritance of God's people, consistent with the gift of salvation she had now received. Along with the promise of an afterlife, she also inherited a role in God's plan of redemption during her lifetime. Ruth was plugged into the

ancestry of the Messiah. This was an unexpected, undeserved privilege of God's grace bestowed upon her among His people.

4. Walked on the Path of Life

As with many of us, Ruth's adjustment was not as easy as falling off a log. In contrast to her life in Moab, she had to live a dependent life in Israel, which was expected. With no male authority in her life in a patriarchal society, and no family or clan, the only way to feed was by gleaning. Gleaning, rooted in the Hebrew practice of 'Laqat,' means collecting, gathering up, or picking up. The custom originates from the Mosaic law, which prohibits farmers from returning to their fields for missed crops. The Torah instructs them to leave these crops for the poor and needy to glean. In its practice, gleaners stationed behind the reapers, gathering the remaining or fallen crops. This is what Ruth was doing. The farmers practised a form of sustainable agriculture, leaving leftover crops on their
fields to provide for the less fortunate. Here, two core principles surface: support for the needy and

the allowance for post-harvest gleaning. Ruth, epitomizing both traits as a poor foreigner, embraced this system. In her

case, Boaz instructed workers to intentionally set aside extra crops for her. This principle is grounded in a deep sense of compassion and fairness towards society's marginalized groups — widows, orphans, and foreigners.

Gleaning embodies the following principles:

1. Observance of the Law: Gleaning at its core is anchored in laws granted by God through Moses to the Israelites. Leviticus 19:9-10 instructs them to leave the corners of their fields unharvested and to gather only what they need, leaving the rest for the poor and strangers. Deuteronomy 24:19-22 also instructs leaving forgotten sheaves and olives for those in need.

2. Support for the Needy: Gleaning provided sustenance for those lacking land or means to grow crops. It ensured even landless individuals could

gather sustenance for themselves and their families.

3. Dignity and Self-Sufficiency Gleaning empowered the poor to take charge of their own lives and strive for self-sufficiency, rather than relying solely on the generosity of others. This approach nurtured dignity and self-sufficiency for the economically disadvantaged.

4. Social Justice: Gleaning in ancient Israel played a crucial role in promoting social justice by addressing wealth inequality and ensuring the fair distribution of resourceswithin the community.

5. Lessons in Generosity: Gleaning taught kindness, compassion, and generosity. By intentionally setting aside portions of their harvest, the landowners cultivated a spirit of generosity and concern for those in need. In summary, the practice of gleaning reflects compassion, justice, and concern for the well-being of the community. It balances dignity and empowerment by providing practical assistance to the underprivileged and encouraging their active participation in securing their livelihoods. The

Bible's historical context emphasizes gleaning's significance in demonstrating faith-based social responsibility.In this new world, Ruth worked as a migrant labourer, her hands stained with the earth as she gathered the leftover crops from the fields. It is possible she missed her old life in Moab, where presumably, she had servants cater to her needs.

But despite these challenges, Ruth's faith in God remained unshaken. She believed that God would provide and show mercy. Her trust in the Lord was not just a fair-weather kind of faith. It was a solid anchor during tough times. Ruth was able to remain steadfast in the face of uncertainties because of her unshakable conviction. Her story is a testament to the fact that faith is not a mere crutch for the easy moments, but it is what empowers us to keep pushing through the challenging times. Ruth's transition from Moab to the fields was more than just physical, it held deep symbolism and spiritual significance. It was a journey of faith, reminding us that relying on a greater purpose can give us strength in the face of difficulties.

***

If you have lived outside God's will and have now chosen to follow Jesus, it is important to have complete trust in Him, even when you find yourself in challenging circumstances that cause others to belittle or ridicule you. Your trust in Him must transcend feelings and be unwavering, knowing that He is faithful and will guide you on the right path. Ruth's love for God was clear, and she recognised that her inheritance in Him went beyond the physical realm. She pursued a spiritual heritage, despite the hunger and lowly lifestyle she had to endure in Bethlehem. Healing from past pain and struggles means being completely free from the negative emotions associated with them and reaching a place where painful memories no longer haunt or torment you. Are you still ashamed of your past? Or do you remember yesterday with gratitude for where the Lord has brought you from? The voice of the spirit encourages us to keep moving forward and avoid the temptation to go back to our old ways.

C. S. Lewis once said: "For God is not merely mending, not simply restoring a status quo. Redeemed humanity is to be something more glorious than unfallen humanity."

Be aware that when you try to leave your past behind, the devil may tempt you with memories of your previous immoralities. If he reminds you of your sinful past, fight back with your future in God. Strike him with your promises in Christ. If you hold on to God's covenant, you will overcome every terrible thing in your past, and He will heal your painful and ugly history. God is able and willing to fashion a glorious future out of your story. Come out of that guilt. Jesus has paid for it. In my experience, the devil used memories of my past to accuse and torment me for years. It caused many sleepless nights, but I held onto God's word and made daily confessions until I found freedom. God helped me. He will help you.

PRAYER
Dear God, I come before you in gratitude for the transformation you have brought into my life

through Jesus Christ. Please help me fully embrace the new lifestyle I have chosen in you. And grant me the strength to let go of old habits and ways of thinking that are not aligned with your will for me. And in moments of doubt, remind me of your unwavering love and faithfulness. Strengthen and empower me to stand firm in my trust in you. Let my life be a testament to your transformative power and grace. In Jesus' name I pray,

ACTION POINTS

1. Embrace Transformation: Just as Ruth wholeheartedly embraced a new way of life, despite her circumstances, commit to letting go of old patterns and adopting a lifestyle that aligns with your newfound commitment to following Jesus.

2. Seek Community: Surround yourself with believers who will support and uplift you on your journey.

3. Practice Patience: Understand that your journey towards complete trust in God might not be instant. Patience is key as you navigate difficult circumstances and continue to rely on His plan..

4. Stay Grounded in His Word: Make it a habit to immerse yourself in the Bible regularly. This will not only strengthen your faith, but also serve as a reminder of God's promises and provide guidance for the challenges you encounter.

CHAPTER FOUR

CATALYSTS FOR FREEDOM:
Restitution, Forgiveness and Reconciliation

Bear with each other and forgive one another
if any of you has a grievance against someone.
Forgive as the Lord forgave you.
(Colossians 3:13) NIV

It is crucial to mention some vital protocols of the new path we have been discussing, as they are necessary steps for making significant progress.

It is essential for believers to go through the steps of restitution, forgiveness, and reconciliation. But it is also important to remember that everyone's life experiences differ, so the specifics of the process will vary from person to person. If your experience of these processes differs from what I am about to explain in this chapter, there is no need to worry. It certainly does not invalidate yours. Even though God has a typical process for dealing with people, His methods vary.

Confess your faults one to another, and pray one for another, That ye may be healed. The effectual fervent prayer of a righteous man availeth much. (James 5:16)

RESTITUTION
Making restitution requires acknowledging the harm caused to others and taking actions to restore what was taken. If we have truly encountered the Lord and received forgiveness for our wrongs, we should aim to make restitution and repair any damage we have caused. Contrary to the erroneous argument of some believers, restitution is not 'works', neither is it an attempt to purchase salvation. Rather, it is evidence of our confidence in God's forgiveness and a mark of genuine repentance.

The concept of restitution is rooted in the biblical principle of justice, which emphasises the need to make things right with those we have wronged. God prescribed restitution to the children of Israel in the Bible.

He says:
Say to the Israelites:
'Any man or woman who wrongs another in any way and so is unfaithful to the Lord is guilty and must confess the sin they have committed. They must make full restitution for the wrong they have done, add a fifth of the value to it and give it all to the person they have wronged. (Numbers 5:6-7) NIV

Evangelist and Bible teacher, Derek Prince gives a definition of restitution in his 1990 book 'Blessing or Curse: You Can Choose' as follows:

"Restitution means to make right any wrong that we have done. It means to take responsibility for our past actions and to do all that we can to make things right. This includes confessing our sins, asking for forgiveness, and making any necessary amends."

Here are some scriptures concerning restitution:
If a man gives his neighbour money or goods to keep for him and it is stolen from The man's house, if the thief is caught, he shall pay double.
(Exodus 22:7)

If a soul sins, and commit a trespass against the LORD, and lie unto his neighbour in that which was delivered him to keep, or in fellowship, or in a thing taken away by violence, or hath deceived his neighbour; Or have found that which was lost, and lieth concerning it, and sweareth falsely; in any of all these that a man doeth, sinning therein: Then it shall be, because he hath sinned, and is guilty, that he shall restore that which he took violently away, or the thing which he hath deceitfully gotten, or that which was delivered him to keep, or the lost thing which he found, or all that about which he hath sworn falsely; he shall even restore it in the principal, and shall add the fifth part more thereto, and give it unto him to whom it appertaineth, in the day of his trespass offering. (Leviticus 6:2–5)

The importance of restitution may have been overshadowed and appeared to have taken the backseat, frequently being associated with the Old Testament and the works of the law. It is just as significant today as it was then. In Matthew 5:17-18, Jesus states that He did not come to abolish the Law or the Prophets, but to fulfill it. This statement carries profound implications for our understanding of restitution. Restitution is a New Testament practice as the Holy Spirit leads one who has accepted the Lord to make restitution where He (God) deems it necessary. Zacchaeus's story is a brilliant example of this.

And Jesus entered and passed through Jericho.
And, behold, there was a man named Zacchaeus,
which was the chief among the publicans, and
he was rich. And he sought to see Jesus who he
was; and could not for the press, because he was
little of stature. And he ran before and climbed
up into a sycamore tree to see him: for he was to
pass that way. And when Jesus came to the place,

he looked up, and saw him, and said unto him, Zacchaeus, make haste, and come down; for today I must abide at thy house. And he made haste, and came down, and received him joyfully. And when they saw it, they all murmured, saying, that he was gone to be guest with a man that is a sinner.

And Zacchaeus stood, and said unto the Lord: Behold, Lord, the half of my goods I give to the poor; and if I have taken anything from any man by false accusation, I restore him fourfold. And Jesus said unto him, this day salvation come to this house, for so much as he also is a son of Abraham. (Luke 19:1-10)

This occurrence shows us that Zacchaeus did not merely repent and turn his life over to the Lord. He responded to the Spirit's nudging in his heart and demonstrated three important actions required for genuine repentance and transformation.

1. CONFESSION

Zacchaeus made a public confession of his belief and declaration of faith. He acknowledged Jesus as Lord and publicly declared his faith. Confession is a crucial aspect of repentance, as it involves acknowledging our sins and turning towards God.

2. RESTITUTION

Zacchaeus was not only repentant but remorseful for his offences. He took practical steps to make restitution by promising to pay back everyone he had defrauded. Restitution is an important part of repentance, as it involves making amends for the harm we have caused.

3. SEEKING FORGIVENESS AND RECONCILIATION

Zacchaeus was willing to seek redress and forgiveness for past offences. He demonstrated this willingness to seek forgiveness from those whom he had wronged and set things right. Seeking forgiveness and reconciliation is an important aspect of repentance, as it involves acknowledging the harm we have caused and taking steps to repair broken relationships.

Zacchaeus' actions demonstrate that genuine repentance involves not only acknowledging our sins and turning towards God, but also taking practical steps to make things right with those we have wronged. Note that Zacchaeus promptly made restitution because the Holy Spirit convicted him of his sins. When a sinner genuinely repents, the Lord, working through the Holy Spirit, will uncover aspects of their lives that require their focus and attention.

WHAT SHOULD A CHRISTIAN RESTITUTE?

The typical question people ask is, "How do I decide what should be restituted and what shouldn't be?" I find that a vital question. Because, while some things are clear-cut, like returning stolen items or owning up to wrongs, not everything is that straightforward, and not everything can be or needs to be restituted. It can be difficult to make restitution, especially when the consequences of past mistakes are irreversible. Imagine someone repenting but unable to find the person they've wronged, or think about sins such as abortion, where it's impossible to revive the baby. It is crucial to recognise that not every sin can be restituted, and attempting to do so would be like to trying to obtain salvation through our efforts, which is futile. Salvation comes through grace because no one can be righteous on their own; no amount of restitution can save you. Only God's grace will.

The Bible highlights the importance of repentance — turning away from sin. As Ephesians 4:28 (NIV) says,

'Anyone who has been stealing must steal no longer but must work, doing something useful with their own hands, that they may have something to share with those in need.'

Therefore, a believer should prioritise repentance, forgiveness, and adjusting their conduct, because they have been made righteous through the gift of 'justification'.

Justification means being declared 'Not Guilty.' You are not guilty, but justified through faith in Jesus'

finished works on
the cross, which is the only payment for sin. So, we do not gain our righteousness through following the Mosaic law but through faith in Jesus Christ, as no one is justified under the law.

Therefore, New Testament restitution does not require adherence to the Law; it involves living by the spirit of life. To ensure consistency in this approach, prayer and following the Holy Spirit's lead are essential when applying the restitution principle. It is not only about restitution "where feasible," but about restitution that is required and guided by the Holy Spirit when we are convicted and prompted to make amends. The Holy Spirit guides believers in making restitution as He places a burden on their hearts. In my case, I could not make amends for every mistake I made, as only the cross would atone for my past sins. I could only repair damaged relationships as the Holy Spirit led me. And first on my list was my relationship with my father.

AUSTIN

After my conversion, I was uneasy about my last exchange with my father. It could hardly be called a conversation, as his final words to me were of rejection, and I responded recklessly by refusing to speak with or visit him. I felt my anger was justified. My ego was hurt, and I vowed never to return to the place where I had been rejected. But I had given my life to Christ, and my perspective shifted. Eventually, I could no longer ignore the inner pull to visit him, so I took a bold step, flung my bruised ego out the door and went home to apologise.

Kneeling before my dad, I asked him to forgive me for the trouble and pain my rebellion had caused and to take me back as his son.

"I am now born again."
"I have changed."
"You'll see that I have changed."

And before my eyes, he softened like butter in a heated pan. News of my conversion had previously reached his ears, but my apology convinced him.

"That is something good to hear," he said without asking me to stand.

"That is a good thing."

I noticed his body language changing as we spoke, becoming more open and receptive. I could see from his expression that he was having more confidence in what I was saying.

"Have you now come home? Or you are going again?"

"No, sir. I'm living in the church now. I am staying in a room they gave us there."

My father was visibly surprised to see me kneel. The Austin he knew would never kneel before anyone. But my actions touched him, knowing my previous tough and uncompromising stance. My heartfelt apology had a significant impact on healing our relationship. He was, however, still sceptical about my decision to stay in the church, so he came unannounced one early morning while I was asleep to see for himself. One of the brothers woke me up, and I saw my dad standing by the door. He stood there briefly, nodding in approval before he left.

You see, you certainly cannot apologise or make restitution for all the wrongs you have done. The Holy Spirit would guide you in the process of reconciliation by highlighting specific things and relationships that need attention. It is important to respond to His prompting when this happens. Apart from my father, I will share some restitutions that God led me to do by His Spirit.

SEEKING FORGIVENESS

You may be familiar with the Filipino proverb which says, "a clear conscience is more valuable than wealth." In my experience, that statement was as true as an apple is a fruit. Even though I had reconciled with my father, I could not shake the strong feeling that I needed to make things right with several other people to have a clear conscience. One act of restitution stands out vividly in my memory; the day I apologised to my ex-girlfriend's mother. Hadiza and I had a wild, rambunctious relationship everyone was aware of. On one of my licentious escapades, I had slept with her on her widowed mother's matrimonial bed. I did not know if Mama knew what we had done, but I felt compelled to expiate my actions because the Holy Spirit put in my heart to apologise. When I went to the house, Mama's face registered a blend of recognition, and yet utter apprehension. I greeted her, then knelt and asked for her forgiveness for what happened between her daughter and me in her bedroom. As we spoke, she affirmed she had heard I was born again, but by my actions, she could validate the authenticity of my transformation. She forgave me and also had something important to tell me. Then she revealed she had not forgotten that day, because, in her revulsion, she had placed a bitter curse on me. Yet I had

no idea. I had no idea that there was a curse hanging over my head from that callous action. My heart ached with an intense weight of regret and remorse. It felt as if a heavy burden was crushing me, making me wish I could dissolve into the ground like raindrops on thirsty desert sand. It occurred to me that the Holy Spirit must have wanted me to apologise for this reason; because a curse was hanging on me.

Speaking in Hausa, she said, *"I was heading towards the room that day, and I overheard the sounds from inside. I instantly knew what you people did. I cursed you."*
"I said you were taking advantage of us because my husband is no

more. And I cursed you that you will never prosper. And you would

never become anything in this life."

"Believe me, I meant everything I said that day." She recounted.

When I was a drug peddler, Mama's home was one of my hiding spots. In addition, I provided them with financial assistance. This is why she concluded I abused my position, showing no respect for her or her deceased husband.

I pleaded for forgiveness, holding nothing back, letting go of any pride I had left. Being fully aware that the curse held, I expressed my regret and brokenness freely and without reservation.

Sometimes, when apologising, individuals are more focused on maintaining their reputation than genuinely seeking forgiveness; have you ever noticed this behaviour in people? That sort of apology might pamper your ego, but it will do nothing to heal the hurt you have caused and can hinder your ability to receive true forgiveness. The key to fixing a broken relationship lies in being able to display your brokenness and remorse sincerely. The next time you find yourself in a situation where you need to apologise, it is important to remember that the two most important things you can do are to be humble and honest.

God is all-knowing and all-powerful. He knew that woman was bitter towards me because of what I had done, and only my apology would heal her heart and liberate me; that was why He led me to her. Yes! Liberate me. I believe I was bound because I was guilty of the offence and it was not until I apologised to her that her heart was healed, and I was finally free from the curse of my offence. The Bible says that "...*whoso breaketh an hedge, a serpent shall bite him.*" (Ecclesiastes 10:8)

But glory to God, I received forgiveness.

It is amazing how a simple act of apology can have such a profound impact. So, if you have broken a hedge and are carrying the weight of guilt, take a step towards freedom today.

Apologise to those you have wronged and let God work in your heart to bring healing and restoration. It is a sure way of letting go and leaving the past behind. And, trust me, it is worth it.

FORGIVING

Are you tired of carrying the weight of past hurts and traumas?

I have been there. At first, I assumed apologising to those I had wronged would be the end of the matter, but it turned out that there was more to the process than I initially thought. It took me a while to realise that letting go of the past meant more than just seeking forgiveness from others. It is also about extending that same grace and kindness to those who have hurt you in the past. Even in cases of abuse, betrayal, assault, or molestation, it is essential to release the burden of anger and resentment to move forward.

It was not until I found my faith and started walking with the Lord that I became aware of the deep-seated animosity I had been holding towards my aunt. I was a victim of her abuse. I had been avoiding this crucial part of my life, so I kept it hidden deep within my heart. I tucked it safely beneath layers of rocks, never to be unearthed. Although I focused on consecrating myself and finding healing and deliverance from my past sexual sins, I also found myself grappling with occasional childhood flashbacks, which I would quickly dismiss. It was not until later that I realised my born-again, forgiven spirit was harbouring unforgiveness.

I was in the university, quite far away when my father invited me home for an important meeting. Aunty Anna, for reasons unknown to me, decided to speak with my parents about the abuse that had taken place. Tears filled my mother's eyes as we sat in the parlour, arms wrapped around her chest in a self-embrace. When I sensed she was blaming herself for the situation, I made a conscious decision not to say, "I told you so," because it would have been pointless and unhelpful.

Meanwhile, my father remained silent, wrapping himself in a cloak of quietude, as a man would cover himself with a blanket on a chilly day.

Quick flashes replayed in my now mature mind; such that disgust and sudden rage welled within me when I glared at her pathetic face. I shook my head as if that would shake off the anger that built up within me. I wanted to ask her what I had done to be exposed to such sheer malevolence. The thoughts stayed in my mind, just like the truth of my abuse remained in my heart all these years. It took more than a decade and

a half for this truth to finally come to light. And it

hurt my heart right down to my soul to look into her face again. The intensity of the pain made it clear that I had not thoroughly healed from the event.

After everything that happened, I was unsure of what kind of relationship I could have with her. But I turned to the love of Christ, and He guided me. One thing I was thankful for was her confession. I was glad she spoke the truth. I forgave her because dwelling on the past is pointless. The Lord told me to give her my cherished possession, a valuable travel bag, as a gift to show my forgiveness. Despite the difficulty, my heart knew it was the right decision, and I could not disregard it despite my anger. I pushed through the pain and carried out the task. For it seemed like a task indeed. It was not until I completed the task that I realised a weight had been lifted from me, a burden I had not even recognised I was carrying. It was a critical period of letting go, and I felt a sense of relief that I had never known before.

The weight of unforgiveness had caused my heart to shatter into a million pieces. But forgiving helped me to heal and put the broken fragments together. Only after truly letting go was it possible to bind those pieces together. Since that moment, I have been able to talk about my past without any sense of guilt, fear, or shame. I was free for real! The Bible says: If the Son, therefore, shall make you free, ye shall be free indeed (John 8:36). Forgiveness frees us from invisible manacles. Forgiveness is essential for genuine healing.

Renowned Christian author, ethicist, and theologian, Lewis Benedictus Smedes made a profound statement about this.

He said:
"To forgive is to set a prisoner free and discover that the prisoner was you."

I believe this statement to be so true. If you have experienced hurt and pain, do you find it difficult to move beyond those feelings? I understand. But it is important to understand that holding on to the pain of the past hinders you from true healing and keeps you tethered to the exact thing you're trying to escape. Think about it; that person you avoid, that issue you do not want to talk about, or even think about, what emotions do they stir up in you? Hurt? Pain? Anger? Resentment? Disappointment?

Do you find yourself holding onto grudges and feeling burdened by negative emotions? Why carry so much weight on your soul? Many experts in the medical and spiritual fields have researched and concluded that unresolved feelings of unforgiveness can be the root cause of several terminal diseases, mental illnesses, and spiritual battles. If you are keeping track of who did what, when, and how, chances are high that your actions are being detrimental to your health. The key to healing is to acknowledge the pain, process the emotions, and let them go. It is not always easy, but it is possible and essential for true healing and freedom. So, take a deep breath, gather your courage, and take that first step towards letting go. For His grace is available.

For me, surrendering to the Lord was the key to my restoration. I knew I could not do it alone. Through His love and grace, I was made whole, inside and out. This is the path to achieving the true freedom we long for.

In Matthew 5:23-24, Jesus admonishes us concerning the need for reconciliation. He says:

Therefore, if thou bring thy gift to the altar, and there rememberest that thy brother hath ought against thee; Leave there thy gift before the altar, and go thy way; first be reconciled to thy brother, and then come and offer thy gift.

Unforgiveness will hinder your prayer and, ultimately, your relationship with God.

If you feel the need to, stop and think about the strained relationships you have and the people you need to forgive; or if you do not have peace with anyone, try to fix it. Take action, make a call, pay a visit, and commit to stop living with the bile. Do not go on relating and replaying the experience to anyone who cares to listen. Forgiveness has benefits for both parties, the one who forgives and the forgiven. It is a powerful tool that has a positive impact on one's mental and physical health, making it a valuable practice for everyone to consider. Forgiveness is found to decrease stress levels and cause a newfound sense of joy and contentment to emerge. I experienced this when I forgave my aunt. Also, when someone receives forgiveness, they feel a profound sense of redemption, and a second chance to mend broken relationships. It is like being given a fresh canvas upon which to paint a brighter picture.

Yet, let us not underestimate the complexity of forgiveness. It does not always unfurl without effort, especially when the offences have been consequential or recurring. When faced with such circumstances, the journey towards forgiveness is likely to be long and require ample time for healing. But it is possible.

There have been moments in my life where I have faced the challenge of forgiveness. This was especially true in the situation with Aunty Anna, where the wounds ran deep. The process required not only a willingness to let go of the resentment I felt but also a journey of understanding and empathy. Like a delicate flower pushing through the cracks in a sidewalk, forgiveness can emerge even in the harshest of circumstances.

However, the cycle of forgiveness is not complete if the offender is unwilling to acknowledge their fault. But for your healing, forgive and receive peace from the Lord even when the person who wronged you has made no attempt at reconciliation or is unwilling to acknowledge their wrongs. This is the tricky part. Pardoning a person does not always mean you will be reconciled. And there is no need for self-flagellation if the other person is unwilling to reconcile. What is most important is that you play your part with sincerity.

The Bible says:

If it is possible, as much as depends on you, live peaceably with all men. (Romans 12:18).

Receive God's abundant grace in Jesus' name.

PRAYER

Dear God, guide me and grant me the grace to heal completely from any childhood trauma or past wounds that may hinder my wholeness and completeness in life, as well as obstruct my walk with you. Please give me the strength to make amends where necessary. Bestow upon me the grace to forgive and to be forgiven by anyone I may have offended. In Jesus' name, I pray. Amen.

ACTION POINTS:

1. **Restitution**: Begin by reflecting on any harm, if any, that you may have caused to others and consider making amends to restore what was taken or damaged. Ask yourself:

• Who has been affected by my past actions?
• Who do I need to have a conversation with to address the past?

• What practical steps can I take to make things right?

2. Seeking Forgiveness: Take time to assess your relationships and identify any areas where you need to seek forgiveness. Be humble and honest in your apologies, showing true remorse and a willingness to make things right. Respond to the prompting of the Holy Spirit in the process of reconciliation. Ask yourself:
• Who have I hurt through my actions or words?
• Are there any unresolved conflicts I need to address?
• How can I communicate my apology without shifting

3. **Forgiving**: Examine your heart for any grudges, hurts, or resentments that you may be holding onto. Understand that forgiving others does not excuse their actions but releases you from the burden of anger and resentment.
Consider the profound impact of forgiveness on your mental and physical well-being. Think on these:

• Reflect on relationships where you hold on to grudges or resentment.

• Who do I need to forgive?

• Reflect on why you should forgive, focusing on your own well-being.

• Approach the individual and express your decision to forgive them.

• Let go of any lingering negative emotions and commit to maintaining a forgiving attitude.

4. **Reconciliation**: Recognise that true healing involves both seeking forgiveness and extending forgiveness. Be open to the process of healing broken relationships, but also understand that reconciliation might not always be possible or depend solely on you.

• Identify a broken relationship you would like to work towards mending.

• Reflect on your role in past conflicts.

• Initiate a conversation with the other person.

• Attempt expressing your desire for reconciliation.

CHAPTER FIVE

A TIME TO GLEAN

I am finally aware, O Lord, that man is not
in control of his destiny and that it is not in
his power to determine the course of his life.
(Jeremiah 10:23) NCB

As we step into the field of Boaz, where love's
journey unfolds, it is vital to understand and
embrace the fact that God is the best guide of your
every step. Finding love among fellow believers is a
beautiful experience, but it requires surrendering to
the Lord's wisdom instead of relying on your own

understanding. He knows better than you do.

Remember this promise: *"For I know the thoughts that I think toward you, says the Lord, thoughts of peace and not of evil, to give you a future and a hope."* (Jeremiah 29:11 NKJV). The Message translation says,

"I know what I'm doing. I have it all planned out—plans to take care of you, not abandon you, plans to give you the future you hope for."

His plan for you is filled with goodness, leading you towards an outcome beyond your expectations. Keep in mind that God's desire for you encompasses finding true love. So, take heart and be assured that as you embark on this journey, His hand is guiding you, and His heart is invested in your pursuit of genuine and lasting love.

In this chapter, I share the story of how I found true love, a love intricately woven into the very fabric of God's eternal plan for my life. Illustrating the role of divine intervention in uncovering God's marital purpose. It is a reminder that true love is not a fairy tale; it is an integral part of our real-life spiritual adventure, where God's handiwork is woven in every twist and turn.

AUSTIN

That day was an ordinary day, remarkable for its unremarkableness. It was a day, like any other, and little did I know it marked the start of my journey with the woman who would later become my wife.

At the time, I was not searching for a companion. I had been there, done that, and I was not ready to commit to a relationship. I was a student and a pastor, and I was not prepared for the 'distractions' a relationship could bring. My previous encounters taught me well.

I moved back home soon after my reconciliation with my father, but continued praying with the brethren in church and travelling for evangelistic crusades with my pastor. I had no plans to go to the university. Zeal for the kingdom had consumed me.

I wanted to immerse myself in God's word and attend a Bible School, but Pastor Moses had ordered us to go to school with some support from the church or find employment within six months. We were welcome to have retreats in church, but the camping period was over! We needed to be, in his words, "useful to society".

So now I was in the university, far away in the Southern part of Nigeria, still on fire for God. I was in my first year at school, and at rehearsal for what we called Fresher's Night at the student fellowship. She was in the choir. We had just finished rehearsing, and I was about to leave. Seated gracefully in the corner near the door, she appeared lost in her own thoughts.

I noticed her.

She did not look like she wanted to be bothered, neither was I interested in bothering anyone, but I heard in my spirit: "ask her name." I refused to go talk to her. Yes, I am one of those who used to negotiate and sometimes argue with the Lord.

"I don't want any trouble. This isn't what brought me here." I thought, responding to His nudging in my heart.

All I came for was to be a part of what was going on that night, so I moved to leave. But I felt the same tug at my heart. I paused. Again, I turned to leave, but a feeling of discomfort sat in my heart. When I felt the pull for the third time, I knew I was being restrained. So, I beckoned to her and greeted her.

"Hello, sister. My name is Austin. Errhm... What's your...name?"

Oh! She immediately charmed me. Her warm, gentle soul was fully captured in her shy smile. She held my gaze in her large, alluring eyes that spoke more than her lips. They looked deep into your core.

"I'm Ebunoluwa. It's nice to meet you."

Since there was not much to talk about, I politely asked her for the address of her hostel and left. She lived in the girl's wing of my hall of residence, Omolayo Hostel. Maybe I could look for her one day. Ebunoluwa had a charming, peaceful beauty I did not forget.

A few days later, my friend, Niyi Owolawi invited me to accompany him to visit some friends. At the door, it was the same room number Ebunoluwa had given me. How serendipitous.

I said: *"Ah, Niyi, this is Ebunoluwa's room nauw."*
"Yes, do you know her?" He asked.

I met his friends, Tosin, Yemisi, Ebunoluwa, who was visibly glad to see me and her younger sister, Comfort. And even though I told Ebun it was purely coincidental, it looked like I had planned the visit. We had a lengthy conversation that day, talking about so many things. Have you ever met someone and felt like you have known them for years, as if they were an old friend? She was the kind of lady with whom you could be yourself. Her eyes lit with pure light; her laughter filled the room, and a soft place in my heart.

Someone in the room was talking about birthday parties. I had never celebrated my birthday. It just did not happen in our home. So, when they asked about my birth date, I casually said August 14.

"Ah! Did you just say 14th August?"
"Are you serious?" She gasped, wide-eyed. "Wow!"
"Wow!"

It turned out we were birthday mates.

There were several other reasons for us to become friends easily. She had a personality that was both straightforward and easy-going. I was funny; she said. She felt like someone I had known for a long time. Being a new student, I was among the first few friends she made, and we regularly spent time chatting after fellowship. And since we had mutual friends, I would visit her sometimes.

As time passed and our friendship deepened, it became increasingly important for us to establish a clear definition of our relationship. We both agreed it would remain a friendly one. Ebunoluwa was like my sister. That was how I saw her, and as such, we were open and frank with each other. Although we both agreed that we wanted nothing serious, we still found ourselves drawn to spending time together. It was easy being friends with someone who had no other plans; only being friends.

Or so we thought.

RUTH

And Ruth the Moabitess said unto Naomi, Let me now go to the field, and glean ears of corn after him in whose sight I shall find grace. And she said unto her, Go, my daughter. And she went and came and gleaned in the field after the reapers: and her hap was to light on a part of the field belonging unto Boaz, who was of the kindred of Elimelech. (Ruth 2:2-3)

It is early spring and time for the barley harvest. As the days grow longer and warmer, the grains change colour from green to a golden hue, showing they are ready for harvest, their stalks wave gently in the breeze. The field is a rich golden landscape filled with long ears of ripe barley - evidence of God's blessing. It is already bustling with activity, as men and women, young and old, stoop over, collecting ears of grain. They have been working from dawn to dusk for many days, yet the fields are still filled with standing barley.

A man stands inspecting the ongoing work from afar, muttering words of gratitude to God for the year's produce.

During harvest times like this, what welcomes you is the scent of dry grain that hits your nose, and the glistening sun-kissed skin of hard-working men and women. As the air fills with the sounds of merriment and music, the reapers diligently bow down, skilfully grasping their sharp sickles or scythes in one hand, and carefully slicing through the stalks that lie low to the ground. Then they tie the stalks up into sheaves and the reapers stack up the sheaves by the side. Afterwards, they leave the gathered stocks to further dry for a few weeks before threshing them on the threshing floor.

In all of this, they leave some margins of the field unharvested. They also do not pick up whatever falls to the ground. This is the norm, and it applies to every harvest - when harvesters grasped a bundle of stalks of grain and cut them with the sickle, as well as when grapes fell from a cluster cut from the vine, and with almonds, figs and pomegranates alike, harvested in the summer.

Boaz observes the activity. Amidst the work, something stands out – someone stands out.

She stands out in the corner of his field, under the blazing sun, with the poise and gait of a stranger he has not seen before. He noticed her. Her conscientiousness moves him, her poise, her carriage, and her chaste conduct as she works among crass men.

"God's peace be upon you," he greets his foreman.
"And upon you too."

"Who is that young lady?"
"Young lady?"
"By the corner."

"The Moabitess? That is Naomi's daughter-in-law. She returned with Naomi from Moab. She asked permission to glean with the others."

"Ruth. Her name is Ruth," another worker responds. *"And she's been out here since dawn,"* he adds approvingly.

Carrying out a most humbling task, Ruth displays admirable traits of both novelty and nobility. She is dignified while being modest. It does not take long for Boaz to notice that she is different from the people around her, and he can easily discern that she has a unique quality that makes her stand out from the rest of the crowd. Her charm piques his interest. This is obvious, for, among other gleaners on his field, Boaz asks only about Ruth. And as if on cue, he saunters towards her and is right by her side.

Clearing his throat, he leans to speak to her.

"Peace and blessings upon you, daughter."

The young lady straightens as her veil curtained her face. Her presence is alluring, yet not Amazonian. As the sun's warmth envelops her, tiny beads of sweat forms on her forehead, resembling a constellation of twinkling stars. These glistening droplets dance toward her sweeping eyelashes.

In the heart of this moment, an unseen destiny unfolds.

But what sets this remarkable journey into motion? It began in the early hours of that morning. Before the sun's first rays paints the sky, Ruth wakes with a hopeful heart, her spirit bubbling with joy. For reasons she does not know, there is a stirring in her spirit. The second chapter of the book of Ruth (in the Message translation) captures the unfolding love story between Ruth and Boaz, and shows how divine plans shape our lives.

One day Ruth, the Moabite foreigner, said to
Naomi, "I'm going to work; I'm going out to
glean among the sheaves, following after some
harvester who will treat me kindly."

Naomi said, "Go ahead, dear daughter."
And so she set out. She went and started
gleaning in a field, following in the wake of the
harvesters. Eventually she ended up in the part
of the field owned by Boaz, her father-in-law
Elimelech's relative. A little later Boaz came out
from Bethlehem, greeting his harvesters, "God
be with you!" They replied, "And God bless
you!"

Boaz asked his young servant who was foreman
over the farm hands, "Who is this young woman?
Where did she come from?"

The foreman said, "Why, that's the Moabite

girl, the one who came with Naomi from the
country of Moab. She asked permission. 'Let me
glean,' she said, 'and gather among the sheaves

following after your harvesters.' She's been at it steady ever since, from early morning until now, without so much as a break."

Then Boaz spoke to Ruth: "Listen, my daughter. From now on don't go to any other field to glean—stay right here in this one. And stay close to my young women. Watch where they are harvesting and follow them. And don't worry about a thing; I've given orders to my servants not to harass you. When you get thirsty, feel free to go and drink from the water buckets that the servants have filled."

She dropped to her knees, then bowed her face to the ground. "How does this happen that you should pick me out and treat me so kindly—me, a foreigner?"
Boaz answered her, "I've heard all about you— heard about the way you treated your mother-in-law after the death of her husband, and how you left your father and mother and the land of your birth and have come to live among a

bunch of total strangers. God reward you well
for what you've done—and with a generous
bonus besides from God, to whom you've come
seeking protection under his wings."
She said, "Oh sir, such grace, such kindness—I
don't deserve it. You've touched my heart,
treated me like one of your own. And I don't
even belong here!" At the lunch break, Boaz said
to her, "Come over here; eat some bread. Dip it
in the wine." So she joined the harvesters. Boaz
passed the roasted grain to her. She ate her fill
and even had some left over.
When she got up to go back to work, Boaz
ordered his servants: "Let her glean where there's
still plenty of grain on the ground—make it easy
for her. Better yet, pull some of the good stuff
out and leave it for her to glean. Give her special
treatment."
Ruth gleaned in the field until evening. When
she threshed out what she had gathered, she
ended up with nearly a full sack of barley! She
gathered up her gleanings, went back to town,
and showed her mother-in-law the results of her
day's work; she also gave her the leftovers from

her lunch. (Ruth 2:2-18)

***

Boaz is well acquainted with the sight of strangers gleaning in his fields during the harvest season, a scene that has become quite familiar to him. Being a Jew, he has extensive knowledge about the practice of Pe'ah, which is like Laqat, but involves leaving corners of his harvest fields for the benefit of the poor, as instructed in Leviticus 19:9-11. Laqat applies to any part of the crops that are left behind or have fallen, whereas Pe'ah specifically refers to the corners of the field. It extends the practice of providing for the poor to include gleanings from the entire field. The Mosaic law distinctly outlined that the corners of fields or farms are to remain untouched, designated for the poor or those unfamiliar to the land to gather from.

In the Orthodox Union (OU) Torah, Rabbi Jack Abramowitz writes:

It is a mitzvah to leave a portion of the field for the needy. This unharvested area is called "pe'ah," meaning a corner. The Torah instructs landowners to allow the poor to take this produce for themselves. Though the Torah only required us to do this for born Jews and converts ("ger," translated "stranger," means a convert), the Sages of the Talmud required that the rule be extended to allow non-Jewish poor to take as well, so there should not be animosity between the Jews and their neighbours.

Boaz is a kind and devout Jew and has kept this law for as long as he can remember. The Lord had implemented several civil laws to ensure that the poor and strangers were taken care of, and this is one of them. These two categories of people — the poor and resident foreigners were unified by their lack of land ownership and thus were dependent on their manual labour for food. Ruth and Naomi fit perfectly into this category. They come back from Moab as poor widows, with little or no possessions, and Ruth is a stranger. So, if anyone had the right to glean in the fields, it would be Ruth.

Boaz, a wealthy man of noble character, greets the woman in the friendliest way and speaks to her softly. Beyond that, he orders his workers to treat her with respect. He ensures that her well-being is taken care of, providing her with a sense of security and comfort.

Of all the fields in Bethlehem, Ruth ends on the Field of Boaz! This was beyond mere happenstance or serendipity; it was a mighty orchestration by the hand of the greatest planner. She had come to Bethlehem in faith trusting the Lord, Ruth trusted God and He directed her path. This would be their first encounter, the beginning of what would soon become their future together.

This is a significant moment in any relationship. I believe first impressions matter a lot. Your first encounter with a person shapes your perception and opinion of that person, and vice versa. You will most likely never know when you meet your spouse for the first time; you cannot plan these things; they are divinely orchestrated.

You could tell that from the moment Boaz set his eyes on her, she caught his attention. As he kept his gaze on her, his interest and intrigue grew. He responded to this stranger in kindness, as was his custom. Somewhere in his heart, he was drawn to this young lady, and did not know why. Yet she arduously focused on seeking to follow the path the Lord had ordained for her, carefully tucking her grief and loneliness beneath her modest smile. Her eyes looked down as though her confidence and strength were on the ground beneath her feet. Boaz felt a tangible connection and wanted to show her yet more kindness.

He was an astute gentleman, a Jew among Jews. He was wealthy, a keeper of the law, righteous, well known - a man of power and character. Boaz kept the law from his youth and was honoured in his estate, upright, showing kindness to strangers and the needy. He was a man of honour, learned in the laws of Moses.

Here was Ruth, a young widow, far too young to be a widow, who followed Israel's God and joined the family of the Jews, fending for herself and her mother-in-law. Hers became a story of total transformation, such that the entire community could testify to her virtue. She was completely unaware that love was around the corner, waiting for her in an improbable place. The same was true for Boaz. As a believer, it is important to trust God and allow Him to guide you (Proverbs 3:5-6). God does not always give man the full vision of where he is leading; He reveals in part. He wants you to submit to His leading and accept Him as the sole guide of your life. By allowing yourself to be led by God's Spirit, you show your faith in God and your willingness to submit yourself entirely to Him while relinquishing your plans.

For as many that are led by the Spirit
of God, they are the sons of God.
Romans 8:14

Trusting in God's guidance may sometimes seem foolish, but it will always lead to the right path.

Although His instructions may sometimes be unclear, if you put your trust in Him and follow His guidance, you will soon see the desired outcome.

When Ruth set out to pick grain from the fields, she did not know whose field it was, and somehow, she ended up in Boaz's field. God's divine direction led her to the right place at the right time, and He positioned her for the right encounter. She yielded to the leading of the Holy Spirit. Ruth may not have been certain of the outcome to expect, but she yielded to what little light she had.

*"I'm going to work; I'm going out to glean among the sheaves, following after **some harvester who will treat me kindly."*** Ruth 2:2 MSG (emphasis mine)

The Bible says, "she **happened to come** to the part of the field belonging to Boaz, who was of the family of Elimelech."

We see God's mighty hand weaving the thread of these lives because they submit themselves to Him. When a man wholly submits to God, nothing in his life happens by chance. There are no mere coincidences, but divine arrangements. It could be something as minor as picking a different route home from work, eating at another restaurant, or stopping by someone's home. As trivial as these decisions seem, they have shaped and made many destinies.

Taking that different route back from work by divine guidance might lead you to discover that opportunity you would not have noticed any other day If you listen to and obey that prompting, it can to guide you towards the breakthrough you have been seeking in your life. For Ruth, it was gleaning in the fields. For me, it began with initiating a conversation with a stranger. What will yours be? You will never know if you do not learn to follow the leading of the Spirit.

PRAYER
Teach me to do Your will (so that I may please You)
For You are my God
Let Your good Spirit lead me on level ground.

(Psalm 143:10) AMP

ACTION POINTS
1. Yield to the Holy Spirit: Ruth's willingness to yield to the leading of the Spirit and act upon the promptings in her heart led her to the start of unexpected blessings.

2. Be open to divine nudges and prompting, even if they seem insignificant. Is there a prompting you have been ignoring or a step you have been hesitant to take? 1Consider yielding to the Spirit's guidance and see where it leads (Job 22:21).

CHAPTER SIX

SPREAD YOUR SKIRT
OVER ME

Then Naomi her mother-in-law said unto her,
"My daughter, shall I not seek rest for thee,
that it may be well with thee? And now is not
Boaz of our kindred, with whose maidens thou
wast? Behold, he winnoweth barley to night in
the threshing floor. Wash thyself therefore, and
anoint thee, and put thy raiment upon thee, and
get thee down to the floor: but make not thyself
known unto the man, until he shall have done
eating and drinking." (Ruth 3:1-3)

AUSTIN
When the Lord revealed my wife to me, Ebunoluwa
and I were just friends, very close friends. We
connected at fellowship and would typically have
prolonged conversations. Although I respected and

cherished her as a friend, I had no intention of pursuing romance. Certain that nothing would develop between us, she was my confidante. She saw me as a brother and a friend. Ebunoluwa was my sister, always open; beautiful, smart, kind, and sweet. And with a laughter that sparkled in her eyes.

One day, whilst on holiday, I was in prayer about the next phase of my life. I was not praying about marriage. Because the last time I did this, I was heartbroken. I still recall that day and how it happened. Without realising it, I had fallen in love with a lady who I was mentoring and counselling.

TOLANI
Although I intended to focus solely on my academics and ministry, Tolani had a peculiar situation. She came from a troubled home, had an absent father, and was struggling with low self-esteem. She confided in me about her family problems, as I taught her God's word to show her His fatherly
love. Tolani's life experience drew me towards her, and I was able to provide her with the support she

needed, acting as a dependable source for her to lean on and confide in. And yet, amid offering guidance and succour, I felt an insidious emotional connection towards her. Empathy grew into a feeling I could not understand, and an inexplicable emotional connection wrapped in intrigue developed in my heart. Maybe it was the nightingale syndrome that made me feel like her knight in shining armour. I cannot say for certain. Either way, I was eager to help her through her troubles. She was the first lady I fell in love with.

Although the Lord had revealed nothing about her or anyone else to me, I knew better than to share my feelings with her. I took my emotions to the Lord. One night, I saw I could not sleep. In the middle of the night, I knelt to pray and opened up my heart to Him, revealing my deepest thoughts and feelings.

"I come naked before you. Naked I was born, and naked I come."

"Lord. I am in love with Tolani. Is she the one?

Please deliver me."

His response was disheartening.

Yet, it was liberating.

"She is not your wife. Your wife is not on this campus."

I cannot fully express the disappointment I felt that night. But at least I knew then I had to restrain my emotions, and I could now focus on my ministry and academics without any distractions. Moreso, I felt a sense of relief wash over me, knowing that I never said a word to her. At least I saved myself some embarrassment. Now that I was sure that my wife was not even in that school, I stopped praying about a life partner altogether.

So, fast-forward to a couple of years later, when I was seeking God's face in prayer at home. I remember I was interceding. I was raised as an intercessor, so that is what I was accustomed to. I was praying for two nations. I was not praying for a wife.

I was not praying for Ebun, either.
But I kept hearing in my spirit:
"She's the one."
"She's the one."
"She's the one."
I questioned, "Who is the one?"
"Ebunoluwa, Grace is your wife."
Bombshell!

Ok. My thoughts were; first, this was not my prayer focus, and second, I had no romantic feelings for Ebunoluwa. Besides, God had told me that my wife would not be in my school, but Ebunoluwa was right there with me at school and on my campus. She was pursuing a diploma course in my school, and she would return for a degree course. Most importantly, I loved her as a friend, but I certainly was not in love with her. It all seemed out of order.

But God reassured me, saying, "Watch and see."
This was one of those moments in my life when I can say I heard God speak in my spirit clearly. I admit, I was slightly confused, but God is not the

author of confusion.

Let me tell you a bit about Ebunoluwa.

GRACE

On the 14th of August, exactly two years after I was born, Ebunoluw (Ebun), Grace, was born in Lagos, South-West Nigeria. In sharp contrast with my experience, she was born into a picturesque close-knit family, a Christian home. Her parents were pastors. In fact, her father was a pastor at the Foursquare Church and later became the General Overseer. Ergo, they raised her with godly standards; she attended the finest schools. More importantly, she got saved at an early age. She was already walking with the Lord as a teenager.

Being friends with her meant I learned a lot from her good-hearted nature. I learnt about the loving father that God is. Even though I had known God to be an all-powerful, all-merciful, patient and kind God, I had not quite known Him as my all-loving Father. My experiences at home did not give me the close father-son relationship I could have used as a reference. So, it was interesting to find out that, after being a pastor for years, I was learning to know that God desired to have a real father-son relationship with me.

Ebunoluwa was a real pastor's kid - well-behaved. Her parents almost completely sheltered her from the troubles of this world. She had a much different upbringing than I did, as she grew up with daily morning devotions and an early lifestyle of prayer and studying the scripture. In a nutshell, she was morally upright. Ebunoluwa is full of virtue in all its colours and shades, an epitome of purity and innocence, all you could ever imagine in a godly woman. Humanly speaking, some people have a clean slate from the very beginning, and my dear Ebun is one of such people. Born in two different locations, under two strikingly contrasting circumstances, like Ruth and Boaz, God's hand was silently and carefully directing my path and hers towards each other.

And now, He had just announced to me she would be my wife!

A time will come in your walk with God when you will have the liberty of the Holy Spirit and the restraint of the Spirit of God. Because you live your life by the instructions of the spirit of God, there are times you will have a release and yet must subject that liberty to the will of God.

I was not praying for a wife when the Lord snuck it into my heart that Ebunoluwa would be my wife. I shared with you earlier that I had no intention of starting a romantic relationship with my now most trusted friend, but it seemed the Lord had a better plan. I accepted His speaking but needed to wait until I got a substantiation to guarantee what I heard. The first thing I did was tell Pastor Moses Akor. He had already heard about her, and Pastor is always excited about growth in the right direction, so he gave me his blessings. He advised me to continue being friends and treat her like my sister. I would let her know soon, but when the time was right. That was one thing that made me know it was a step in the right direction. The fact that the Lord had spoken to me about the person who would be my wife and my mentor was one hundred percent sure I had heard correctly.

But...
God also said, "Your wife is not on this campus."

Like Mary, I kept thinking, how shall these things be? "Watch and see." He said.

But...I was not in love with her. I kept thinking, how can I marry someone that I am not in love with?

"Watch and see."

Back then, we did not use smartphones. People sustained communication across distances through telephone calls from phone booths and through letters. Ebunoluwa and I indeed exchanged quite a number of letters. I would receive hers in the mail and write an immediate reply from Sokoto to Lagos.

Once I was back at school, because I was part of the leadership team of the student church we both attended, I communicated my perceptions to the leadership and got a go-ahead. Ebun and I were part of a group called 'The Reconciliation Team' where we engaged in ministry together, thus she was an active part of my life. But for some odd reason, I still kept these things in my heart, away from her. Perhaps I was not yet ready. I cannot tell you why I stalled. As I delayed, my friend, who was the lead pastor of our fellowship, approached me to say that God had spoken to him and told him that Ebunoluwa was his wife.

Ah!

I encouraged him to go ahead and speak with her about his convictions, without disclosing mine to him. Maybe this would be my litmus test to prove if the Lord had spoken to me or not, and settle all the confusion.

I am saying this because when we believe we have heard from the Lord, we need to dot the i's and cross the t's. It is important for us to be thorough when we believe we have received a message from the Lord; paying attention to even the smallest details. Here we were, two young men on fire for God, 'hearing' His voice regarding the same lady. Hmm.

But God is not the author of confusion.

To cut the story, he spoke with Ebunoluwa. She declined. Then soon after, his fiancee returned, and he went back to her, convinced he had not heard God correctly. I got the assurance I needed to speak with my wife to be. Still, I did not.

It is all too easy for us to take certain relationships for granted and not move swiftly in the direction God is leading us. We may stall around the friend zone for too long and get complacent.
This is not good.
So, this lady that God told me will be my wife soon left my school because she was unable to secure admission for a bachelor's degree course. We kept in touch by exchanging letters regularly. I have

some of those letters to date! Yet I still had not told her what I knew. Fortunately, Ebun visited my school with some other Reconciliation Team members who had graduated. They made the trip to attend a program we organised. Ebun also needed to get her academic transcript certificate from my school to be eligible for a Direct Entry admission to another institution.

Things were falling into place. And I knew I needed to pay attention to this instruction from the Lord. But I was still concerned that there was no romantic attraction to her. As soon as I found out that she did not gain admission into my school, I felt even more certain that God's message about her being my wife could be coming true.

I started praying.
"Lord, I really like Ebun, but I don't love her like that."
"I am not attracted to her."
"Lord, you know I can't marry a woman I do not find attractive...
I will obey You, but I will trust You to plant her love

in my heart
before I ever talk to her."

But the Lord had his own timeline, and I knew this was the time to talk to her, regardless of whether the feelings I desired were present. That night, amid the excitement of getting things set for our programme, I told her to come over for lunch the next day. To bolster my confidence, I reached out to my friends for moral support.

The next day, I made lunch and was seated outside my room, washing up a few things. The moment she entered the compound, I lifted my eyes to see her, my gaze met hers. As I gazed upon her, I realised that this lady was the epitome of beauty. I had never seen her that way. She had such beautiful eyes. In a split second, my mind changed, and I knew without a doubt that the Lord had furnished her love in my heart. I was falling in love with her.

My heart raced with the sudden and unexpected realisation of my love for her, like a thunderbolt striking me. I believe only God can explain how a deep love developed in my heart towards her. My heart raced as I saw Ebun, my sister, my friend and confidante, transform into a stunning woman I knew I wanted to be with forever. God had spoken, and He planted deep love for her in my heart, right there.

I got up, quickly rinsed my soapy hands, and wiped them dry with a towel, then went to hug her. She melted under my embrace. I could neither find my voice nor feel my feet. If I was not sure about anything in my life, I was sure she was the one I wanted to spend the rest of my life with. Although I did not mention it, my heart felt warm towards her. This was my sister, my friend, but today, it was different.

We went in to have lunch. I had prepared a meal of rice, vegetable sauce, fish, and a bottle of fizzy drink. During our conversation in my room, she shared she had been getting interest from several guys. She had already decided to say yes to someone and was enroute to him when God told her to return home because he was not her husband. That was all the prompting I needed. And when she said that, I felt shaky all over. I knew this was the moment. Making up a quick excuse, I dashed out for moral support from my friends, Tunji Akosh and Tunji Savage who were waiting in the room next door. I had lost my comportment. My knees buckled beneath me. This was unlike me. I was not afraid to speak with her, but the transition in my heart was too rapid. From liking someone to feeling a deep love for her. It was all too much for my mind. Pulling myself together, I went back. I wanted to speak the right words. My speech began with me recounting how I cherished her friendship and admired her character. I did not want to sound spooky spiritual. I wanted to speak candid words.

"Ebun. We've been friends for long now, and you've become my sister..."
"I have loved you as a friend. Now I love you...Now I'm in love with you." And...I love you."

"I want you to marry me."

I promised her two things: I will stay faithful to her, and I will take her around the world. Her eyes bore into mine, and there was a pregnant silence in the room.

"You're not saying anything." I said to her.

With a blank stare, she looked at me and said: "I have heard you."

RUTH
And she went down unto the floor, and
 did according to all that her mother-in-law bade her. (Ruth 3:6)

Ruth enters the threshing floor with a pounding heart and clammy hands. She is unsure what will happen by the end of this night, but she knows her mother-in-law will never give her the wrong counsel. She had a bath and anointed herself as Naomi instructed. Mild perfume hangs about her like a soft cloud. She is waiting, waiting to put their plan into action. Naomi has advised her not to reveal herself until Boaz, their kinsman, had eaten and drunk his fill and laid down on the threshing floor for the night.

So, she waits.

Behind her veil, she waits.

It is a little after midnight now. She peeks in. The light emanating from the fire burning at a small distance from where Boaz lay covered with a warm fleece blanket on the hard floor faintly illuminates the room. With the sound of the wind rattling the fire in the room, Ruth creeps towards him and lays at his feet before pulling the cover off his feet.
The room is filled with stillness, except for the gentle snores escaping from his slumbering body. She remains sleepless and nervous as a cat. Ruth observed intently as he attempted to get comfortable by tugging the covers up over his feet, which had grown cold. Then his foot touches something. Something warm. Something real and alive. Something that was not there when he went to sleep. He jerks awake. That something was a woman curled up at his feet!

"What is this?" He shouted, slightly alarmed.
"Who are you?"

The voice that responds out of the darkness is both strange and faintly familiar, scared yet determined.

"I am Ruth, your handmaid: spread your cloak over me, for you are a near kinsman."

***

Ruth's life took a turn when she gave her heart to the Lord and left her people to travel with Naomi to a land where Naomi would be the only person she knew. Her mother-in-law became her mentor, her pastor, from that day. Knowing little about the Jewish faith, she had signed up to follow Naomi's instructions for life.

By now, through Naomi's motherly wisdom, she had learned to conduct herself in piety and dress, putting in mind the laws of modesty, she had guided her in many things until now. Naomi had led her through the customs and traditions of her new community. By now, Ruth knew Naomi had her best interest at heart. But this instruction seemed like a dangerous adventure. Yet, she trusted her mother-in-law's voice and did not question. And this was not the time to turn back. Only trust would make Ruth obey. All she said was, "all that you say, I will do". She promptly responded without question. Naomi understood that part of her role as a teacher to Ruth was to help ensure she took the right path in life.

My brother, my sister, do you have a mentor in your life? Someone to guide you, to lead you when you need to make a major decision? Can you recognise the Lord's voice when He speaks to you? Do you know and trust His voice to follow, even when it does not sound reasonable? Can you follow the voice of God even when you do not know where He is leading?

It is God's desire for every believer to follow only where He leads them, with no deviation. In verse one of the third chapter of the book of Ruth, we see Naomi's good intentions to find rest and security for Ruth.

I love how the Message translation puts it:

"My dear daughter, isn't it about time I arranged a good home for you so you can have a happy life?" (Ruth 3:1) MSG

It is God's will for you to find the rest and security that marriage offers. So, Naomi instructed Ruth to prepare herself, make herself known to the man most suited to be her husband, to bring her to her place of marital rest.

And who was best suited for this position than Boaz, their close relative? He was obligated by Mosaic law to marry her, since she was the childless widow of his relative, Mahlon. That is why she pointed to the fact that he was a near relative, potential kinsman-redeemer.

Let us discuss the role of the kinsman-redeemer.

The Hebrew term for this phrase is (go el). It denotes, next of kin, and, hence, redeemer, one who delivers or rescues (Gen 48:16, Exodus 6:6). The next of kin performs any duty which his near male relative could not carry out before his death. He also inherits his rights and responsibilities. Also, the next of kin's chief duty was to be the avenger of blood if someone outside the clan killed his near relative. The duties of go'el also included redeeming his relative from slavery if sold to a foreigner or sojourner (Leviticus 25: 47-55). He was to raise offspring for his kin if he died with none (as in the case of Mahlon) to follow the principle of the Levirate Marriage prescribed in Deuteronomy 25:5-6, Genesis 38:8.

On this basis, Naomi sent Ruth to Boaz, her kinsman-redeemer, to make herself known to him.

Well, this is not your typical boy meets girl romantic tale. Reading this portion of scripture on the surface, we may be quick to conclude that Ruth was throwing herself at Boaz, making advances toward him. Or attempting to manipulate him. But that was not the case. And if you are a lady reading this and you think I am asking you to kneel and propose to that brother, this is far from it.

Naomi's counsel to Ruth appears suspicious on the surface, and some scholars have explained this action as having ulterior motives; Naomi saw beyond that. The objective of this action was that Naomi wanted Ruth to be married and find rest. It was her attempt to get the attention of a man positioned by the laws of that time to step up as her kinsman redeemer.

Her approach was not nuanced. Rather, it was more simple, cultural and ceremonial than it was coquettish. "Spread the corner of your garment over me" - a symbolic action to show that he would care for her as her husband. This might only seem strange to us because of our cultural background and the ideology of our time.

Mathew Henry captures this in his commentary as follows:

We found it very easy, in the former chapter, to applaud the decency of Ruth's behaviour, and to show what good use we may make of the account given us of it; but in this chapter, we shall have much
ado to vindicate it from the imputation of indecency,
and to save it from having an ill use made of it;
but the goodness of those times was such as saved what is recorded here from being ill done, and yet the badness of these times is such as that it will not justify any now in doing the like.

Henry goes further to say:

... It was a convenient time to remind him of it, (i.e., his responsibility, emphasis mine) now that he had got so much acquaintance with Ruth by her constant attendance on his reapers during the whole
harvest, which was now ended; and he also, by the kindness he had shown to Ruth in smaller matters,

had encouraged Naomi to hope that he would not be
unkind, much less unjust, in this greater...

...Naomi therefore orders her daughter-in-law to make herself clean and neat, not to make herself fine
(v.3): "Wash thyself and anoint thee" not paint thee (as Jezebel), "put on thy raiment" but not the attire of a harlot, and go down to the floor.

By examining Boaz's reaction, we will understand how this was more of a graceful gesture, which he well appreciated:

"The Lord bless you, my daughter," he replied."This kindness is greater than that which you showed earlier: You have not run after the younger men, whether rich or poor. (Ruth 3:10) NIV

This is how the Message translation shows their exchange:

She said, "I am Ruth, your maiden; take me

under your protecting wing. You're my close

relative, you know, in the circle of covenant

redeemers—you do have the right to marry me."

He said, "God bless you, my dear daughter!

What a splendid expression of love! And when

you could have had your pick of any of the young

men around. And now, my dear daughter, don't

you worry about a thing; I'll do all you could

want or ask. Everybody in town knows what a

courageous woman you are—a real prize! You're

right, I am a close relative to you, but there is

one even closer than I am. So stay the rest of the

night.

In the morning, if he wants to exercise his

customary rights and responsibilities as the

closest covenant redeemer, he'll have his chance;

but if he isn't interested, as God lives, I'll do it.

Now go back to sleep until morning."

(Ruth 3:9-13) MSG

According to Boaz, what Ruth did was an act of kindness towards him. She showed no interest in flirting with younger men. She did not take her request to them. Rather, she showed him this kindness by choosing him. By her actions, she let him know he was trustworthy. Trustworthy because she was not afraid that he might take advantage of her. Being a righteous man, Boaz interpreted Ruth's action as kindness, submission, and respect because they meant those to him.

Matthew Henry further explains:
She knew Boaz to be not only an old man (she would not have trusted to that alone in venturing her daughter-in-law so near him), but a grave sober man, a virtuous and religious man, and one that feared God. She knew Ruth to be a modest woman, chaste, and a keeper at home.

In addition, it is crucial to understand that Ruth's behaviour was motivated by the recognition that Boaz had a responsibility as the kinsman-redeemer to protect her and claim her as his own.

And he said, Who art thou? And she answered, I am Ruth thine handmaid: spread therefore thy skirt over thine handmaid; for thou art a near kinsman. (Ruth 3:9)

Note her response, "...spread therefore thy skirt over thine handmaid..." Why? "...for thou art a near kinsman." The simplicity of the 'why' is what caused her to take action, and it is the driving force behind her action. If he were not a near kinsman, she would not be there in the first place. The law had put him in a position he was not even aware of. Ruth did nothing more than let him know his place.

Ruth did not only present Boaz with the opportunity to marry a wife; she gave him the chance to possess her family's estate. So, what happened here? Did Naomi send her on a journey to possess what the Lord had for her? The Lord, in His infinite wisdom, had made this provision for her long before she would know because He promised that *"none shall be barren in the land, and none shall want her mate."*

As Matthew Henry comments, Naomi referred her daughter-in-law to Boaz for further directions. When she had thus made her claim, Boaz, who was more learned in the laws, would tell her what she must do.

She had sensed a new season on the horizon and was leading her into prophecy. Naomi seemed to be saying to Ruth, "a new season is coming for you, an end has come to mourning, bereavement and lamentation." She was to bathe and anoint herself, put on some perfume, beautify herself. This was not possible during her time of mourning. Naomi's words were filled with hope and motivation and I can picture her telling Ruth "You've made it this far, and now it is time to take the next step. The Lord has plan for you that goes far beyond where you are now. Do not let grief and sorrow hold you back anymore. You will go for all that God has for you and not settle for less."

We all need that persistent pastor or mentor who gives us that push to press into God's will. We need someone who would push us into seasons of restoration and transformation. Someone who would provide us with the right counsel, review our choices without undue emotion or bias, and lovingly tell us the truth even when it is tough to hear.

PRAYER

Dear Lord, order my steps in your will.
Lead me in the way that I should go in Jesus' name.
Amen.

ACTION POINTS:

1. **Embrace Divine Timing**: Are you rushing or dragging your feet on your romantic journey? Put your trust in God's perfect timing and His plans for your love life. Just like Ruth, prepare yourself for the right opportunities that God will bring your way.

2. **Step Out of Your Comfort Zone**: Are there chances for love that you have been shying away from because of fear or complacency? Break free from your comfort zone and boldly pursue the path that God is guiding you toward. Just as Ruth followed Naomi's unconventional advice, have faith in God's direction even when it pushes you out of your comfort zone.

3. **Listen and Obey**: Ruth's obedience to Naomi's counsel transformed her life. Similarly, prioritize hearing God's voice and faithfully acting on His

prompting, even if it feels unconventional or challenging. Are there aspects of your romantic journey where you sense God's nudge but hesitate to respond? Trust His leading and take steps of obedience. Obeying God is the path to breakthrough.

4. **Recognise Divine Appointments**: Ruth recognised that God strategically placed Boaz, a kinsman-redeemer, in her life. Pay attention to the people and opportunities that come into your life, recognising that they may be divine appointments. Approach your interactions with an open heart, understanding that God is using them to shape your journey.

5. **Trust Beyond Feelings:** Ruth's story highlights how our feelings can change in unexpected ways when we trust in God's plan. God can stir emotions at the right moment, even if they do not align with our initial expectations. Love can grow in your heart if it is God's will, even if you
do not feel it now.

PART TWO

213

CHAPTER SEVEN

THE SPOUSE THE
LORD GIVES

And it came to pass at midnight, that the man was afraid, and turned himself: and, behold, a woman lay at his feet. And he said, Who art thou? And she answered, I am Ruth thine handmaid: spread therefore thy skirt over thine handmaid; for thou art a near kinsman. And he said, Blessed be thou of the Lord, my daughter: for thou hast shewed more kindness in the latter end than at the beginning, inasmuch as thou followedst not young men, whether poor or rich. And now, my daughter, fear not; I will do to thee all that thou requirest: for all the city of my people doth know that thou art a virtuous woman. (Ruth 3:8-11)

Marriage is not merely a social construct or a traditional human arrangement. It is a unique institution. It serves a sacred purpose that transcends our desires and needs. If we can grasp and embrace this concept, it will make our search for a life partner easier and more fulfilling. For one, it shifts our focus beyond the superficial and mundane to the purview of God's will. And when we look at things, we will do so through the lenses of vision, divine purpose, and assignment. When we acknowledge the sacred origin and purpose of marriage, we shift our focus away from self-reliance towards God's providence. The more we surrender control, the more we open ourselves up to unforeseen possibilities and cultivate a sense of patience in the unfolding journey. Instead of relying on our human wisdom and intellect, God's word and His Spirit become our search engine.

Taking a closer look at Boaz's intriguing encounter with Ruth on the threshing floor, we see so much character and virtue in the interactions between the two of them, and that is my focus in this chapter.

Imagine the surge of panic that must have coursed through him when he saw a figure near his feet. Little did he know, as he retired to his bed alone, that an unexpected presence would soon find its way to snuggle at his feet in the darkness. Trembling, perhaps even wondering if he might be in danger, he found himself face to face with a woman like Adam's encounter with Eve in the book of Genesis.

Adam was unaware of the void that a woman could fill in his life. He dedicated himself wholeheartedly to his divine calling of tending to the garden. God, however, understood his essential need for companionship. And while He remained focused on his purpose, a life-changing encounter awaited him.

When we steadfastly pursue our divine assignments, the Almighty intervenes, orchestrating the fulfilment of our deepest desires. And on a day like no other, as the sun cast a golden glow across the garden, Adam awoke, astonished to find a figure beside him. Here are his exact words:

This is now bone of my bones and flesh of my
flesh: she shall Be called woman, because she
was taken out of man. Therefore, shall a man
leave his father and his mother, and shall cleave
unto his wife: and they be one flesh.
(Genesis 2:23-24)

Adam discovered in Eve a piece of himself that he did not even realise was missing. In Ruth's case, however, Boaz was startled, but her soft trembling tone reassured him.

"I'm your servant Ruth. Please cover me with your robe."

Pay attention to these significant words: kinsman, threshing floor, cover.

What Ruth did was a symbolic act of espousal—symbolising her availability for marriage. Consider this:

- She dressed to impress him, not in the attire of a seductress.
- She lay humbly at his feet, not beside him.
- She was asking to be covered, not undressed.
- She was inviting and presenting him with a token of
  matrimony, rather than a mere physical affair.

She was saying, cover me, protect me, spread your garments over me, and put me under your wings, for you are my close relative. What we see here is like what happened in the sixteenth chapter of the book of Ezekiel. We see God speaking to Israel as her 'Husband', her Redeemer, the one who covers, using similar words.

I passed by you and saw you, and behold, you

were at the time for love; so I spread My skirt over you and covered your nakedness. I also swore to you and entered into a covenant with you so that you became Mine," declares the Lord GOD. (Ezekiel 16:18)

The passage describes God's commitment and protection of Israel as He spreads His mantle over her and espouses her to Himself, similar to how a man proposes to a woman with an engagement ring today. Similarly, when Ruth requested Boaz to provide the same level of commitment, she was following the customs of her time. Her goal was commitment. She was
making herself available for an espousal, so she extended an invitation. The Bible says she lay at his feet until morning. As the sun rose in the morning sky, before anyone could catch a glimpse of her and tarnish her reputation, Boaz asked her to return home, though not without a glimmer of hope and assurance.

Following Divine Direction

I have seen many well-meaning believers jump lock, stock and barrel into terrible relationships, and, ultimately, wrong marriages because they use improper methods of choosing a life partner, or they judge with incorrect parameters. To make the right decision, it is important to combine the guidance of God's word, the leading of the Holy Spirit, and sound judgment. While God may not always specifically pin-point a prospective spouse for you, He must definitely have a say in your choice.

As with other areas of our lives, God provides instructions, guidance, and suggestions for our potential life partner. However, He does not forcefully dictate our choices. He respects our freedom to choose. He does not impose His will on us because He values our free will. It is just in the same way that He offers His salvation to us and yet allows us the freedom of choice in accepting this salvation. And as God offers His love to us, giving us the freedom to accept or reject it, He grants us the same freedom in selecting a life partner, because genuine love cannot exist without the freedom to choose. Although God may not necessarily handpick our spouse, He plays the role of orchestrating situations that bring potential partners into our lives. The story of Ruth and Boaz shows this through God's subtle suggestions and opportunities for them to meet and fall in love.

Isn't it fascinating that some believers receive divine guidance in various aspects of their life, including that of others; yet even some highly spiritual individuals have made regrettable decisions in selecting a life partner? This emphasizes the importance of seeking the leading of God's Spirit to make the right decision in this crucial aspect of our lives.

God has given us the precious gift of His spirit within us. He is our guide. He leads us on the path we should go by the sense of life and peace He furnishes in us. Yet He has also given us a significant responsibility - the power of free will or choice. Hence, we possess the ability to make decisions and are ultimately accountable for the choices we make.

I believe Adam had the choice to accept or reject Eve, the same way he had an option to obey or disregard God's instructions about the tree of the knowledge of good and evil. God gives us this freedom of choice, but it is limited within the company of believers because if we have indeed given ourselves to Him, our choice should emanate from Him. He leads and guides, but eventually, we make the choice. So, the Lord may lead you in one direction, and you may decide to go in the opposite direction.

In Genesis 24, we witness the intricate process of finding a spouse for Isaac. Abraham, a wise patriarch, entrusted his servant Eleazer with a vital mission: to seek out a bride for his beloved son, Isaac. With specific instructions in hand, Eleazer embarked on his journey, filled with anticipation and hope. However, the ultimate decision rested in the hands of Rebecca and her family. It was within their power to accept or decline the proposal. If Rebecca's father, Bethuel, had chosen to refuse the offer, the course of the story would have been altered. Similarly, Rebecca herself had the freedom to reject the offer presented to her when she was asked, *"Will you go with this man"?* And she willingly said *"Yes"*. Genesis 24: 49-67

And Abraham was old and well stricken with age, and God has blessed Abraham in all things. And Abraham said unto his eldest servant that ruleth over all that he had, "Put, I pray thee thy hand under my thigh and I will make thee swear by the Lord, the God of heaven and the God of the earth, that thou shall not take a wife to my son, of the daughters of Canaanites with whom I dwell. (Genesis 24: 1-4)

Abraham was communicating the principles of the kingdom that he had learnt from God. He revealed that there is a realm within God where one can seek and find a suitable life partner. It is essential to understand that marriage should not be dictated by external factors such as ethnicity or nationality, but rather by kingdom affiliations. Being Yoruba does not
limit you to marrying only within your tribe; likewise, being Canadian does not restrict you to a

Canadian spouse. And your spouse does not need to be Igbo simply because you are Igbo. Our compatibility in relationships is not determined by our natural tribal affiliations, but by our spiritual alignment and shared direction in Christ Jesus. The bonds we form with
our life partners transcend cultural and ethnic boundaries. In Genesis 24:5. Look at the instruction of Abraham to Eliezer

And the servant said unto him, peradventure the woman might not be able to follow me to this place. Must I need bring thy son unto the land whence thou cometh from?" And Abraham said unto him, "Beware that thou takest not my son there."

As far as Abraham was concerned, it was far better for Isaac to remain single than return to Mesopotamia. It is wiser to stay single than compromise your faith for marriage. If someone will lead you to disobey God, then they are not in alignment with His will for your life. Recall the words of Boaz to Ruth: *"...From now on, don't go to any other field to glean—stay right here in this one."* (Ruth 2:8-9, MSG). Here, we encounter a vital lesson. Boaz specifically uses the word 'stay,' which in Hebrew is 'dabaq' meaning to cling or join closely. In the Septuagint translation, it is translated as 'kollao,' which signifies to glue or be joined to. Boaz urges Ruth to stay close, to cling to him and be united with his maidens rather than seeking provisions in another field. This highlights the importance of remaining committed and connected to those who are aligned with God's

purpose for our lives.

You should be prepared to follow the instructions that will come from God at any time so, we no longer live by explanations, but by instructions. Many times, we try to help God accomplish what He has promised us, and we end up getting it wrong. When He makes a promise, it is captured in the spirit. And it is only by the spirit we see its manifestation. We cannot achieve God's promises by our physical abilities or in the flesh; for the Bible says, *"For as many as are led by the Spirit of God, they are the sons of God."* Romans 8:14.

And He will lead you in the way you should go. But you must go in that way.

Who you find during the searching period can make or break a successful marriage. As the famous Benjamin Franklin once said: "Keep your eyes wide open before marriage, half shut afterwards." The quote stresses the importance of being discerning and observant when choosing a life partner. Before entering marriage, we must pay attention to the qualities, values, and compatibility of our potential partner. I think it is important to consider certain factors when choosing a life partner.

First, what are some of the biblical values that are exalted in the woman, values to which our men must pay attention when they seek a blessed union?

THE VIRTUOUS WOMAN
Who can find a virtuous woman? For her price is far above rubies. (Proverbs 31:10)

These words, written over 3000 years ago, still ring true today, as virtue remains a timeless topic. Men who are searching for a wife should prioritise having realistic expectations, rather than chasing after an idealized picture of a partner. My brother, finding a wife, is not about making an unrealistic checklist of superheroine qualities and going around with a magnifying glass, meticulously analysing every woman you meet to see if she checks all the boxes. That is unrealistic and unnecessary.

Let us look at some biblical qualities you need to look out for in a woman.

1. INNER BEAUTY

Let us face it, if there were such a checklist, beauty would often be at the top for many men. Do you agree? And while I do not undermine the importance of beauty, it is equally essential to consider virtues and qualities that will contribute to a strong and healthy partnership. You know, they often say that marrying someone just for their good looks is like buying a house because of the paint colour.

There is a lot more to a person than meets the eye. Beauty certainly matters, but here is the thing: beauty is subjective. What one person finds attractive, another might not. It is important to remember that when you are on this search; you need to shift your focus beyond the surface allure and physical appearance. They should not be your only driving force. Look beyond the surface of a woman and focus on qualities that truly matter, such as character, compatibility and shared values. Because in the long run, it is those inner qualities that will make your relationship beautiful and fulfilling.

2. A WOMAN WHO FEARS THE LORD

Ruth was not only stunning, attractive, and hard-working, she possessed an exceptional quality that set her apart - she was a woman of virtue. Given the circumstances, Ruth could have been many things, but she chose the path of virtue and piety, showing high moral standards in the face of hardship. The Bible says,

Charm is deceitful and beauty is passing, but a woman who fears the Lord, she shall be praised." (Proverbs 31:30) NKJV.

Ruth's example of beauty and unwavering virtue inspires us to value character and seek a woman with a deep reverence for God. A virtuous woman fears the Lord and displays godly qualities in her conduct and character. She cannot be bought, and her worth is far greater than any material possession. Proverbs 31:10 asks, "Who can find a virtuous woman? For her price is far above rubies." For a woman like this, money alone cannot win her love; you need something more valuable. I understand the significance of material possessions, but what I mean is that a virtuous woman values the more important things in life. To such a woman, true love is not just about gifts, but about the giver. Boaz showed kindness to Ruth, providing her with food, drink, and abundant grain. While she appreciated his gestures, she desired something more precious—she wanted him. True love surpasses material possessions, for its yearnings delve deeper than mere gifts. True love craves the presence of the giver.

Look out for a woman who values you for who you are, not just what you can offer.

3. A WOMAN OF DILIGENCE
Being industrious is another remarkable quality of a virtuous woman. Diligence goes beyond mere hard work; it is rooted in an inner strength that perseveres through challenges. Her deep reverence for God serves as the foundation for her inner strength and diligence.

Proverbs 31:13 and 16 say,
She seeketh wool, and flax, and
worketh willingly with her hands...

She considereth a field, and buyeth it:
with the fruit of her hands she
planteth a vineyard.

Her diligence shines brightly, whether she is managing responsibilities or making crucial decisions. She is not just completing duties; she's infusing them with dedication. She embodies unwavering commitment and a determination that stems from a deep well of faith. Diligence is not confined to tasks; it is a reflection of how someone approaches life with purpose and resolve. She is your steadfast companion during challenges, using them as opportunities to grow. And you can trust that she will be your pillar of support, unwavering in her encouragement. If you are seeking a meaningful relationship, keep this in mind. Just as a woman's diligence mirrors her devotion, her commitment to nurturing your relationship will radiate with similar fervour.

These are some of the qualities that a man should look out for in a lady, qualities that the Bible exalts. A godly woman brings immense blessings and joy to a marriage, and by choosing a virtuous woman, a man sets the foundation for a strong and fulfilling relationship. My brother, look for a woman who holds a deep respect for God and takes her faith seriously, as her spirit radiates her inner beauty. I cannot emphasize this enough. Inner beauty is what will stand the test of time. A man should seek a lady who exudes beauty from within.

A WORTHY MAN
Now Naomi had a relative of her husband's,
a worthy man of the clan of Elimelech, whose
name was Boaz. (Ruth 2:1)

Many times, we find ourselves heavily focused on
encouraging women to develop the qualities of an
ideal partner for marriage. However, this emphasis
can sometimes cause us to unintentionally overlook
the equally vital conversation about the attributes
of a good man.

Often, we focus heavily on the need for women to
develop themselves into that virtuous woman who
is desirable for marriage, whilst we overlook the
importance of discussing the qualities of a faithful
and worthy man. In the same way, we have said so
much about the nobility and virtue of Ruth without
shining the spotlight on Boaz. So, let us shift our
perspective a bit. As we look deeper into the book

of Ruth, we find Boaz as a shining example of a godly man who embodies the characteristics of a suitable spouse. The first time we meet him, we are told of his character and pedigree, 'a worthy man of the clan of Elimelech'. Furthermore, the initial words he speaks reveal important insights into his persona. He said 'the Lord be with you', demonstrating his strong spiritual foundation. He believed in the Lord enough to bless people in His name, as was common with noble Jewish men. When a person's foundation is rooted in godliness, it influences even the very words they speak. This godliness is a crucial trait to seek in a potential suitor and should never be compromised.

Whilst the Bible does not specifically outline the qualities of an ideal man in a single chapter, as we see in Proverbs 31, the Bible however, offers numerous pointers that describe the characteristics of a godly man. Let us explore these qualities in the following paragraphs.

1. THE FEAR OF THE LORD
And behold, Boaz came from Bethlehem.

And he said to the reapers, 'The Lord be with
you!' And they answered, 'The Lord bless you.''
(Ruth 2:4)

Blessed is the man who fears the Lord.
(Ps 112:1)

Dear sister, the first thing a godly woman should
consider when seeking a suitable spouse is the fear
of the Lord. Ask yourself, does he fear God? And if
you are honest with yourself, you do not need to
think too far to answer this question, because a
genuine fear of God is evident in a person's lifestyle.
I always say that when a man truly fears the Lord, it
has a profound impact on every aspect of his
character. "The fear of the Lord is the beginning of
wisdom." That is so profound. The fear of the Lord
is the foundation upon which all other virtues and
qualities and strength of character are built. When
a man walks in alignment with the fear of God and
acknowledges His authority over his life, he will
naturally follow God's will. This would guide every

decision and action he takes in life.

2. INTEGRITY
Whoever walks in integrity walks securely, but he who makes his ways crooked will be found out. (Proverbs 10:9) ESV

A man of integrity is one who stands firm and holds on to his convictions, even when he has an opportunity to compromise. A man of integrity will not compromise God's standards. Dear sister, no woman should be involved with a man whose words are shifty, who says one thing now and a different thing later. Integrity is critical, especially in our day and time when people say one thing and do something else. A suitable spouse is a righteous man, godly, and full of integrity; he is a man who keeps his word (Proverbs 20:6-7). A suitor should be faithful and trustworthy in everything.

I remember there was a couple whose marriage was on the brink of falling apart when the wife discovered her husband's premarital deception. During their courtship phase, the husband had portrayed himself as a high-ranking staff member in a prestigious organisation, driving several cars, which naturally impressed her. She fell for his façade. However, shortly after their marriage, cracks began to appear in their relationship. They started facing financial difficulties, and frequent quarrels erupted. She felt that he was not meeting her needs and was withholding his earnings from her. Meanwhile, in reality, he was just a driver with a meagre salary. Unable to bear the weight of such deception, the lady contemplated divorce.

Mendacity or dishonesty can create deep wounds and fracture the foundation of trust that is crucial for a healthy partnership. Look out for this.

3. HONOUR
And she lay at his feet until the morning: and she rose up before one could know another. And he said, Let it not be known that a woman came
into the floor. (Ruth 3:14)

Boaz saw a vulnerable woman lying at his feet, yet he displayed great godliness and integrity. Instead of taking advantage of her vulnerability, he addressed her with utmost respect and referred to her as 'my daughter'. He did not prey on her, neither did he take advantage of her vulnerable position. He committed himself to treating her with dignity and care. Boaz demonstrated a genuine concern for preserving her honour and chastity. He understood the potential social consequences that Ruth might face if it became known that she had been on his threshing floor. Boaz was concerned about how she would be seen in the eyes of society should anyone see her leaving his threshing floor.

Dear sister, is your beloved careful to protect your honour? Or does he insist on shredding it? Is he insisting that you stay over and spend the weekend so that you "know each other better"? It is important in any relationship to have a partner who values and protects your honour.

A person who genuinely cares about your well-being will not pressure you into compromising situations or rush the relationship beyond what is appropriate. Instead, they will prioritise going through the proper channels and seek guidance from the appropriate authorities, ensuring that the relationship progresses in a respectable and responsible way. Boaz waited until he met the appropriate authorities and went through the proper channels. He did not want to take the relationship to the 'next level' until it went through the right process. Boaz was concerned about Ruth's integrity and his honour too. He did not want to taint her image and have himself perceived as one out of order.

Does brother 'XYZ' want you to keep your relationship secret because nobody should know or because he wants to go through the proper channels of authority? Is he urging you to keep the relationship secret without valid reasons or transparency? Does he want you to keep quiet because he has a plan up his sleeves?

Similarly, it is important to evaluate whether your partner's desire for secrecy aligns with a genuine commitment to honour and respect, or if there may be underlying motives or plans that are not in line with healthy relationship practices.

Boaz acted orderly in propriety and according to established laws.

4. KINDNESS
He measured six measures of barley, and laid it on her: and she went into the city...
(Ruth 3:15b)

Boaz displays so many good reasons for giving to Ruth. His generosity shows his kind-hearted nature, his love and acceptance towards her. Love gives and giving is God's nature.
Boaz was bent on protecting her honour. He clearly stated that he did not want her to return home empty-handed. This gift is intended for Naomi as Ruth's parental figure, signifying his recognition of her home and of her family.

I have come across women who would purchase gifts for their mothers in the name of a suitor, intending to preserve his image and reputation before their family. However, in the end, they are only deceiving themselves.

5. COMMITMENT

...as the Lord lives, I will redeem you.
(Ruth 3:13)

I understand that people's circumstances differ, as with relationships, but I need to state this clearly. Ladies, it is crucial to reflect if a man is not actively pursuing marriage and commitment. If he is not making efforts towards marrying you, either by committing himself to you, by his words, or taking steps towards advancing your relationship, you should sit back and think. If he avoids conversations about the future or shows indecisiveness, it is time to contemplate moving on. Do not invest in a relationship where marriage is just an option. Remember, you deserve someone who chooses you with conviction, not hesitation. Recognise your worth and prioritise your happiness and well-being in your relationship. If a man shows a lack of commitment towards marriage, it is crucial to take a step back and reflect on the situation. Relationships should be built on mutual respect, trust, and shared goals, including the desire for a committed and fulfilling partnership.

You should not take choosing a life partner lightly, as it is a significant decision. It is important to scrutinize potential suitors and evaluate their intent. Choose someone who is enthusiastic about the relationship, communicates honestly about the future, and is devoted to the Lord.

Dear brother and sister, the decision of whom to marry is of utmost importance, as it has the potential to shape your entire life. Making a mistake in the choice of a life partner can have long-lasting consequences and significantly impact your overall well-being and happiness. Give careful thought to this decision, for it has the power to shape the course of your entire life.

You know, I once saw an inscription on a T-shirt that read: 'I told my wife to embrace her mistakes and she hugged me.' I took two things out of that. First,

I am glad I would never need to own a shirt like that. Second, every woman should diligently scrutinize any suitor who comes to her until she is certain of his person so that she would not need to embrace a life-size mistake.

PRAYER
Heavenly Father, please open my eyes to see beyond the superficial. Open my ears to hear beyond mere words. Open my heart to embrace the spouse you have prepared for me.

ACTION POINTS:
Embrace Divine Timing: Are you rushing or dragging your feet on your romantic journey? Put your trust in God's perfect timing and His plans for your love life. Just like Ruth, prepare yourself for the right opportunities that God will bring your way.

CHAPTER EIGHT

DOES MY CHOICE
MATTER?

If you abide in Me, and My words abide in you,
you will ask what you desire, and it shall be done
for you. (John 15:7) NKJV

DOES MY CHOICE MATTER?
Yes! Your choice matters. After all said and done,
you will live with your spouse, not God. Remember,
God does not shove his choice down our throats, so
it is your responsibility to seek His will for your life
and find someone who aligns with that.

I cannot guarantee that you will always have your way; you need to yield to the Holy Spirit. This is typified by what Ruth did when she cleaved to her mother-in-law constantly receiving counsel from her. Even after her sister Orpah left, she was determined to be under her mother-in-law for life. Marriage begins when you die to yourself and the flesh. The scripture says, *'Except a corn of wheat falls to the ground and die, it abides alone.'* (John 12:24). The responsibility of finding a wife indeed rests on the man as the scripture says, *'he who finds a wife...'* and not *'he who receives a wife'*. However, it is still the Lord who determines what your preference for a wife would be. In certain circumstances, He even uses his sovereignty to pinpoint the exact woman as in the case of Hosea (Hosea 3:1). Because you can never truly know someone completely; it takes the revelation of the Spirit to see someone for who they truly are. *'Wherefore henceforth know we no man after the flesh...'* (2 Corinthians 5:16).

FINDING THE ONE

So, who can find a virtuous wife? As we have already established, you cannot find her on your own. 'Her worth is more than rubies' Money and physical appearance cannot buy her. Just as you cannot discover divine revelation in the Word without spending time with God, you cannot find a virtuous woman outside of God. 'Every good and perfect gift comes from above.'

Have you ever wondered if God's will would match your desires? The very thought of this is a bit daunting, isn't it? The person who is God's will for you may not initially be your heart's desire, and I say this carefully. It may not all be romance in the beginning. This person may not possess all the qualities you have in mind. They might not even be your type. However, God knows you more than you know yourself and sees a future you cannot see. He can stir your heart to develop feelings for an unlikely person if you are open to Him. The key is to be certain of His will. Sometimes, we find love in unexpected places. It is the nature of love. I knew some sophisticated ladies on campus. Ladies who walked as though they glided along on gentle winds.

A few years later, they got married to men who did not look like the perfect picture. Men who did not seem to match their level of sophistication. You would not have believed that those ladies would respond to a mere "hello" from men like that, but there they were, married. Conviction happened.

THE DANGER OF DESPERATION
It is important to recognise that life is not solely about preparing for marriage. Unfortunately, some individuals, when they reach a certain age or status, become overly fixated on finding a soul mate. They obsess over finding a life partner and view marriage as the ultimate goal, neglecting their personal growth, career, and overall happiness. Their goal in life is to get married, sometimes at all costs. Yet they have not even scratched the surface of what God has in store for them.

An anonymous quote resonates this deeply: 'Marriage is not the destination; it is merely a chapter in the grand story of your life. Do not make it the entire plot.' This quote encapsulates the truth that God has created each individual with a unique purpose and calling that extends beyond the context of marriage. Our ultimate goal should be to fulfil His purpose for our lives, a purpose that He ordained even before the world began. The only thing the Bible admonishes us to live in preparation of is the coming of the Lord (Matthew 24:44).

There is a common belief that marriage is all about finding that missing piece, your soul mate, or someone who completes you. But let me share a different perspective with you. Marriage is not solely about finding someone to complete you. It is so much more than that. It is a profound union of two individuals who come together to complement each other to fulfil God's divine agenda. As Ecclesiastes 4:9-10 says, 'Two are better than one because they have a good return for their labour: If either of them falls, one can help the other up. But pity anyone who falls and has no one to help them up.' When two people come together, they can achieve greater success. Marriage is a partnership where a man and a woman come together to establish His will on earth.

We live in a world that often romanticizes the idea of finding a perfect soul mate. Let us challenge ourselves to shift our perspective. Instead of tirelessly seeking someone who fits every specification, let us focus on finding ourselves. Personal growth and self-discovery should be our focus. Let us strive to be the right person, someone who is whole and complete in God. In doing this, we open ourselves up to a life of fulfilment and purpose.

Here is something important to remember. You are most ready to enter a relationship when it comes without stress; with a sense of peace and contentment, rather than desperation and urgency. Do not rush into a relationship when you are solely preoccupied with finding a partner. I realise that overly desperate people usually end up settling for less than they deserve, far from what is truly best for them. Constantly being consumed by the need to find a partner may inadvertently cause you to overlook important red flags or compromise your standards. Rushing into a relationship, solely because you are fixated on being in one, can lead to settling for less than what God has in store for you. Desperation can cloud your judgment and prevent you from recognising when a relationship is not healthy or fulfilling.

So, my friend, let go of the notion that marriage is about completing yourself or finding the perfect soul mate. Embrace the moment, embrace the journey of personal growth, trust in God's plan, and be patient. The right person will come into your life when the time is right. Focus on becoming the best version of yourself, and watch as God orchestrates the beautiful story of your life. Embrace the process of becoming the best version of yourself and trust that the right person will come into your life at the perfect time. As you focus on personal growth and rely on God's guidance, watch as He weaves together a beautiful story that exceeds your wildest dreams.

Do not be compelled to go into a relationship under duress; it should come without stress or the sense of urgency. It is when you have a sense of peace and contentment that you are most ready.

Desperation and a sole preoccupation with finding a partner can cloud your judgment and lead to settling for less than you deserve. When you are constantly consumed by the need to be in a relationship, important red flags may go unnoticed, and you may compromise your standards.

Let me share a story about a friend of mine Jane. Jane reached a point in her life where she felt the pressure to get married, because all her friends in her church group were walking down the aisle, and she began to fear that she would miss her chance to have children, worrying that she will become too old. In an effort to help her, we rallied together to find her a suitable partner. After a few months, a mutual friend introduced Jane to a man who seemed like the perfect match. He was a successful businessman and a Christian, precisely what she had been looking for. Their connection was immediate and strong. They hit it off right away, maybe a little too quickly. They were both mature individuals, deeply committed to their faith, or so it seemed. You would think it would be smooth sailing, right? So, what is the worst that could happen?

Not long after, however, red flags surfaced. The man started exhibiting signs of his old habits, maintaining contact with ex-girlfriends from his pre-Christian days, which raised concerns among us. Worried about Jane's wellbeing, we approached her and shared our worries. Surprisingly, she brushed off our concerns and responded,

"It's because we're not yet married. Once we are married, he'll change."

"There is no time to waste time."

I believe we even became a nuisance to her. Our intentions were genuine, but she saw us as an interference rather than a source of support. To make a long story short, Jane eventually had to move back to her parent's house with her two children, unable to bear the pain of her husband's infidelity. Her experience serves as a stark reminder that individuals may present themselves as Christians, but their past struggles can resurface unexpectedly.

Reflecting on Jane's journey, if she had heeded our advice and resisted the urge to rush into marriage, her story might have unfolded differently. The lesson here is simple: do not allow yourself to be swept up in the pressure of time and the fear of missing out. Take the time to know and understand someone before entering such a life-changing commitment.

If you are feeling pressured or rushed into a relationship, these feelings serve as clear indicators that you may not be ready. In those moments, take a step back, breathe, and remind yourself that it is not a race against time. If you are not prepared to embrace a relationship with a calm and open heart, then it is not the right time for you. Relationships should never be entered into out of desperation or the fear of getting older. Such mindsets are not conducive to building healthy connections. Do not rush the process or let external pressures cloud your judgment. Instead, approach relationships with a solid foundation of readiness and genuine desire. Remember that marriage should be a beautiful addition to your life, not a desperate attempt to fill a void. Only the Lord can truly fill the void within us. Take the time to discover who you really are, pursue your passions, and become the best version of yourself. When you are at peace with your identity and direction, you will be in a better position to attract the right person into your life.

HOW TO KNOW YOU ARE NOT READY

Certain motivations may indicate that we are not ready for this lifelong commitment. And, my brother, my sister, you know you are not ready if you find yourself in any of these situations.

1. If you want to marry to prove a point:

Proverbs 21:2 reminds us that while we may think our ways are right, the Lord weighs our hearts and knows our true motives. Marrying to prove a point reveals a self-centered mindset, lacking the selflessness needed for a loving marriage. It shows you are indeed not ready to be married.

2. If you want to marry to get back at someone else
perhaps, an ex:
Seeking marriage to get back at someone, especially an ex, is not only a foolish idea but also self-deception. Such a move will lead to pain and disillusionment.

3. If you want to marry to escape your present condition:
If you see marriage as a way to escape your current circumstance, it can result in unhealthy relationships and feelings of disappointment. This perspective indicates that you may not be ready for the lifelong commitment marriage entails. Instead, focus on finding contentment and personal growth in your present situation, so that you are prepared to form a strong partnership. Marriage should not be used as a means to run away from challenges but rather as a foundation for facing them with your spouse.

4. If you want to marry because you feel you are getting old and running out of time: Feeling like you are getting old and running out of time is a common concern. However, rushing into marriage is not the solution. Remember, God's timing is perfect, and He knows what is best for you. As (Psalm 31:15) NIV reminds us, 'My times are in your hands.' I love that scripture. Simple, straightforward, and true! Trusting in His timing brings comfort and assurance that He knows what is best for us, so there is no need to be anxious about running out of time. Instead, find peace in knowing that He will guide you and fulfil His purpose for your life in the perfect time and season. So, if you feel the pressure to get married because you are getting old, take a deep breath, trust in God's plan, and enjoy the journey without rushing into something that may not be right for you.

5. If you want to marry because you feel you have been in the relationship for too long:
The feeling that you have been in your current relationship for too long, or you feel too attached to

turn back, is still no reason to rush into marriage. Take a step back and consider if the relationship has achieved its goals and if you are both prepared for the lifelong commitment of marriage. Remember, marriage is a marathon, not a sprint. Prioritise building a strong foundation and ensuring compatibility before saying "I do." Rushing into marriage based solely on relationship length can lead to challenges and unmet expectations in the future. In Ecclesiastes 3:1 (NIV), it says, 'There is a time for everything, and a season for every activity under the heavens. Seek God's guidance and wisdom to determine the right timing for marriage. Relationships are a journey of growth and discovery. So, while at it, maintain an open communication, assess your readiness, and align your goals and values. Do not let the duration of the relationship dictate your decision to marry. Instead, trust in God's timing, and when the time is right, you'll be better prepared for a fulfilling and lasting marriage.

6. **If you want to marry because you need financial assistance:** Is a change of financial status your motivation for wanting to get married? If your

answer is yes, your perception is flawed. Marriage is about purpose, not money. Proverbs 19:14 (MSG) says, "A congenial spouse comes straight from God." Choose a partner based on love, compatibility, and a shared purpose. Do not rush into marriage for financial gain. Instead of focusing on financial motives, prioritise what is most important. Do not rush into marriage if money is your primary motivation. It shows you are not ready.

7. If you want to marry because you want to please others:
Am I now trying to win the approval of human beings, or of God? Or am I trying to please people? If I were still trying to please people, I would not be a servant of Christ." Galatians 1:10 (NIV). This scripture pretty much sums it up. If you prioritise the approval of people rather than the will of God, you are putting yourself in a position as a puppet on a string, where your actions and decisions are controlled by external expectations. If this is your plan, you are not ready to get married.

8. If you want to marry because you want to satisfy sexual lust:
You want to be married solely to satisfy sexual lust? That is not a good idea, my friend! While physical attraction is important, very important, it should not be the only reason for wanting to get married to someone. Let us confront those lustful urges head-on, because what happens when they arise in marriage? Do we start planning another marriage? You see what I mean? Lust is a problem to tackle head-on, with prayer, God's word, and the help of the Spirit. Trying to solve lust with marriage is like trying to cure greed by feeding a greedy person more—does not work, right? 'He that hath no rule over his own spirit is like a city that is broken down, and without walls.' Proverbs 25:28. The real issue lies in self-control and learning to bridle our desires. If you want to get married for any of these reasons, or some other form of pressure, you might not be taking the right step; marriage is a lifetime commitment. It is an enormous step to take; a decision that needs to be handle carefully and wisely. In the meantime, I advise you to keep pursuing fulfilment in God. Become firmly rooted in

Him, pursue godly, platonic relationships, and enjoy being alive for the sake of fulfilling your purpose in God first.

PRAYER

Dear Heavenly Father,

Guide my heart as I seek a partner for life. Help me to embark on this journey of marriage through your eyes, valuing character and alignment with your will. Open my heart to your divine guidance and grant me patience to wait for your timing. May my relationship reflect your love and purpose. In Jesus' name, amen.

ACTION POINTS

1. Reflect on Your Perspective on Marriage: Does it align with God's perspective? Is your focus on a divine purpose, or is it on personal desires and societal norms? What areas do you need alignment? Dive deeper into this reflection by journaling your thoughts and feelings about marriage. Write your beliefs, fears, and expectations. This introspection will help you uncover any misconceptions that will hinder your journey towards a God-centred

marriage.

2. **Evaluate Your Preferences in a Spouse**: What do you look out for in a potential spouse? Contemplate whether these qualities are significant to a lasting marriage. Are these preferences in alignment with God's principles and the divine purpose of marriage?

CHAPTER NINE

PROPOSAL

And he said, Who [art] thou? And she answered,
I [am] Ruth thine handmaid: spread therefore
thy skirt over thine handmaid; for thou [art] a
near kinsman. (Ruth 3:9)

I know this is an exciting topic for many, especially
in this day and age where proposals are becoming
more and more unique and interesting. It is like a
competition to see who can come up with the most
creative idea! When it comes to proposing, there is
no one-size-fits-all approach, so feel free to get

creative and do it in a way that resonates with your beloved.

Have you heard about the latest trend of interrupting an entire church service to propose? Hmm, now that takes some boldness! But imagine the commotion if the answer turns out to be a "no." Usually, at this point, the brother better be sure before causing a church-wide commotion! Ultimately, what matters most is that your beloved accepts your heartfelt proposal, regardless of the approach you take.

The key thing is the question and the reply that follows. When you are certain you have found the right person and you believe it is God's will for your life, you can get down on one knee and pop the question, as they say. How you do it is entirely up to you as there is no prescribed order for a proposal.

You may choose to kneel in a busy airport, maybe place rose petals on a trail, or even hide a ring in a bowl of ice cream (just make sure it does not get lost in the mix). Whatever works for you. A certain brother wrote an epistle, another serenaded with a guitar and sang the words. There was even a creative soul who made a custom puzzle with the words 'will you

marry me?' when completed. The answer to that question had better be a "yes", otherwise, all the time put into that puzzle would come to waste. I imagined this one guy who tied the engagement ring to a heart-shaped balloon and presented it to his damsel. When he got on one knee to propose, as her eyes widened, she put her two hands over her mouth and let go of the balloon, which sailed up to the sky. Needless to say, they had to buy another ring.

That was not my experience. I did not need to purchase another ring. In fact, I did not even propose with an engagement ring. Instead, I had to wait. I waited patiently for her response. I waited for so long, days turned into weeks, weeks turned into months and in the end, I found I had waited for more than a year for Ebunoluwa to accept my proposal. When I presented my heartfelt 'manifesto' to her that unforgettable day in my room, all she said was, "I have heard you." And in the context of finding a life partner, that response could hardly be regarded as a definitive "yes." It was not even a "maybe." Later, I discovered that when I proposed to her, and she responded the way she did with that historic blank stare, it was because she felt that I had allowed her to go on and on about several other people that were asking her out. She planned to say yes to one of them, but God instructed her not to and told her not to enter any relationship until her final year in the university.

So, when I came with my proposal, she questioned why I did not act sooner and why I allowed her to tell me about her suitors. She had to head back to her school, but a few days later, I got a call from her. She told me it was fine for us to stay friends, but she needed some space and preferred not to be in touch for a while. Ebun did not mention how long the break would be.

She said, "We can remain friends, and you will always be like a brother to me. But please, I don't want you to call me. Don't call me, don't text. I need some space."

I was devastated.

This happened right before my semester exams. Ebun was a principled lady, and she was firm in sticking to her principles. Although I initially protested, saying that friends should call each other, I respected her decision and gave her *"space"*.

During the exams, I could not concentrate because of the emotional turmoil. Till date, it remained the most difficult exams I had written. But she kept her word as I knew she would. She neither called, nor did she respond to my calls. When the exams were over, I travelled to Ibadan, South-West Nigeria, and paid her a surprise visit at her school. I expressed how her actions affected me during my exams, and we had a heartfelt conversation. I recall some things I said, "The way you treated me was not just bad; in fact, it was quite cruel. You didn't consider my feelings at all, and you didn't even care that I was in the midst of my exams. Did you think that was fair?" I pressed my point. "Didn't you realize how badly your actions would affect me? And indeed, they did, in case you don't know." These were some of the things we spoke about on that visit, and she apologised.

However, Ebun still did not say "yes," so I went back to Lagos.

Back in Lagos, I bought her a new mobile phone to replace her old one, which was malfunctioning. However, she adamantly returned the gift, saying she could not accept an expensive gift from me when she had not officially said yes to my proposal. This made me admire her more, as it showed her lack of materialism.

Despite the uncertainty in our relationship, I needed to know my fate. Other ladies on campus were showing interest in me. A couple of them had even mentioned that they had visions and dreams that I would be their husband, but I knew Ebun was the one for me. Despite my attempts to get a hint or a concrete answer, she stayed firm and insisted there was no answer Meanwhile, somehow, perhaps by intuition, I already had a feeling that whatever her response would be, she would choose our birthday, August 14th, to share it with me. And I was unconsciously looking forward to that day. So, on August 14th, 2002, I was in Sokoto and she was on holiday in Lagos during her final year at the university. I received a call from her and she said, "I want to talk to you today." I must admit, my heart skipped several beats as I held the phone, waiting for her to decide my fate, this lady I now loved with all my heart.

She began, "I am surrendering my life to you. I accept your proposal, not just as a husband, but as a mentor, a pastor, and a father."

Phew! A heavy sigh eluded me.

"Are you there?" she asked because my silence lingered.
"I'm here," I finally managed to say.

Then I reminded her of my fears.

"Do you remember I told you that after all you've put me through, waiting for you for so long, not knowing where to place you in my heart and unsure of where you placed me, I might not have much excitement left if you said yes?"

I continued. *"Well, okay...that's fine. Thank you. The Lord will help us."*

WHO SHOULD PROPOSE
When it comes to the question of whom to propose, it is important to consider what scripture has to say on the matter. While the Bible does not explicitly state who should take the initiative, we can gain insights from its teachings.

In Proverbs 18:22 (NKJV), says, *He who finds a wife finds a good thing.*

This scripture suggests that it is the man who takes the
proactive role in seeking a partner. The scripture says, "He who finds a wife..." not "she"... Therefore,

the word of God emphasizes that it is the man who finds the wife, not the other way around. And through a careful study of the Bible, we can observe certain patterns and principles.

In many biblical accounts, we see men taking the initiative in seeking a wife. We rarely see a man propose to a woman directly. Usually, he goes straight to her family (father, brothers or relatives) and seeks their blessing before entering a covenant. This approach highlights the significance of familial relationships and honour within the context of marriage. We will discuss this later. Additionally, when Adam was created, it was said that a man would leave his father and mother and be joined to his wife (Genesis 2:24). This suggests a sense of responsibility for a man to take the lead in the marital journey.

Call me old-fashioned, but I still subscribe to the proper way of doing things. Many ladies these days choose to propose to a man. I have even heard of those that kneel before the man. Scripture clarifies the gender that does the "finding" (Proverbs 18:22).

The Bible says in Genesis 2:24,

Therefore shall a man leave his father and his mother and shall cleave unto his wife.

Now, this does not mean that women cannot show their interest or make themselves available. We have seen from the story of Ruth that this is possible. As she positioned herself before Boaz, making herself known to him and informing him of his position as her redeemer without proposing. As a lady, sometimes the reason you are still single is not that you are not *'wife material'*, it is because you cannot be *'found'*.

The key is to balance being approachable and respectable. Making yourself available does not mean parading yourself before every man or compromising your values. No! That is a manifestation of a seductive spirit. It is the man's job to find you, but if you keep hiding, you may never be located. It is about being gracious, confident, and displaying godly virtues that attract the right person. It is best for you to come out of hiding. Put yourself out there, graciously, with all virtue and confidence. Make yourself approachable, yet respectable. You can be courteous and pleasant without being prurient. Bear in mind, the objective is not to be seductive or to seek attention without discretion. It is the man's responsibility to take the lead in finding you, but you can play a role by coming out of hiding and positioning yourself in a way that allows a genuine connection to happen. While cultural practices may have evolved, it is valuable to consider the biblical principles and patterns for proposals and courtship. The foundation of any relationship should be built on the love, respect, and commitment shared between both individuals.

Prayer:
Dear Jesus, I ask that you grant me wisdom and guidance as I navigate this path of love and relationship. Help me find the right person and to have the patience to wait for your perfect timing. I will not miss it in Jesus' name.

ACTION POINTS

1. **Balance Approachability and Respect**: If you are a single lady desiring a relationship, focus on balancing being approachable and respectful. Work on being confident, gracious, and virtuous while making yourself known to potential suitors. Position yourself in a way that allows for genuine connections to develop.

2. **Take that Step of Faith:** As a man, is there someone on your heart whom you believe you are meant to propose to? If the Lord has guided your steps thus far, gather your courage, seek His guidance in prayer, and make that proposal. He has led your journey, and He'll continue to light your path.

3. Embrace God's Plan: Dear sister, if the Lord has brought a brother into your life and you sense His hand in it, do not hesitate or waste time. Embrace the opportunity that God has presented. May you find the grace to respond with clarity and confidence, aligning your decisions with His purpose. In Jesus' name, may your choices reflect His guidance.

CHAPTER TEN

COURTSHIP AND ENGAGEMENT

"Two are better than one; because they have a good reward for their labour. For if they fall, the one will lift up his fellow: but woe to him that is alone when he falleth, for he hath not another to help him up." (Ecclesiastes 4:9-12)

COURTSHIP

Courtship is a Christ centered relationship geared towards marriage, where both individuals are rooted in purpose, prioritising intentional spiritual growth, prayer, and careful planning for a future built on God's design. By now, the man must have had a direct conversation about his intention to marry the lady, going beyond simply expressing love: and there is a mutual commitment to embark on the journey of marriage together, leaving no room for doubt or speculation. At this stage, there is only one purpose to the relationship: MARRIAGE.

The courtship period is crucial, as it gives the couple time to build their relationship further. During this period, the couple need to invest time and effort in building a solid foundation for their relationship. It is the time to;

• fortify the foundation for the marriage and strengthen commitment to each other.
• spend time together and deeply get to know one another.
• seek the will of God regarding His purpose for the marriage.
• build a solid foundation based on shared values and a common purpose.
• have deep conversations.

In courtship, couples should have deep, meaningful conversations about their values, goals, and dreams, fostering a deeper connection through open communication. With Christ as their cornerstone, they lay the groundwork for a strong and enduring union.

For Ebunoluwa and I, we had moved from the friend zone, but being apart presented a challenge, as we were no longer in school together. We no longer had the luxury of time to talk as we used to when we were just friends. Heartfelt messages and letters became a precious way for us to communicate, bridging the distance and expressing our love and commitment. And, in those days, there was an amazing thing called 'midnight calls'. A mobile phone company allowed subscribers to make free phone calls from midnight till 4:30am, called 'extra cool'. It was a blessing, especially for long-distance relationships like ours. Those midnight calls became our lifeline, allowing us to talk for hours without worrying about the cost.

Those nights were a precious time for us to connect, share our hearts, and strengthen our bond.

Courtship requires commitment because the ultimate objective of courtship is to lead to marriage. Period! Marriage is the mutual goal that the two people both intentionally and actively pursue. At this stage, even though you are still single, you are now exclusive. You cannot be in a courtship with your potential spouse and remain available to others. Courting multiple people simultaneously is not allowed. The way you behave and carry yourself during courtship lays the groundwork for your future marriage. Hence, it is crucial to exercise caution regarding what you allow into your life and what you accept from your partner. If there is a lack of devotion or faithfulness during courtship, it may continue in marriage unless there is divine intervention.

BENEFITS OF THE COURTSHIP PERIOD
The courtship period is truly special and brings many benefits to a couple. It is like a learning ground where you both grow, as Proverbs 27:17

says, 'iron sharpens iron'.

Let us explore a few more advantages:

1. **A Time of Preparation**: During courtship, you have the chance to dedicate yourselves exclusively to each other and to God. It is a season where you walk in faith, hope, and, most importantly, love. Love is the real deal here! This period helps you discover deeper aspects of yourselves, including flaws that might not have been obvious at first. It is about getting ready for a strong and healthy future together.

2. **Deepening Intimacy**: Courtship allows you to genuinely get to know your partner on a whole new level. You see beyond the surface and discover who they truly are. It is like peeling back the layers of an onion. Spending more time together can reveal a different side of what seemed perfect in a casual or friendly relationship. It is an opportunity to grow closer and understand each other more intimately.

3. **Mutual Growth and Support:** Another wonderful thing about courtship is that it gives you both the chance to improve yourselves and help each other grow. Think of it as sanding the rough edges of wood to make it nice and polished. Work on any weaknesses or unpleasant aspects of your lives with genuine love and care. It is a time to encourage each other, just as 1 Thessalonians 5:11 says,

"So encourage each other and build each other up." (NLT)

4. **Shared Values and Goals:** The courtship period allows you to align you values and goals as a couple. It is a period where a couple should have meaningful conversations and discover if their aspirations for the future are in alignment with each other. Sharing the same vision and purpose strengthens your bond and sets the stage for a fulfilling marriage.

5. **Stronger Emotional Connection:** Through courtship, you have the opportunity to build a deep emotional connection with each other. Spending quality time together, opening up, and sharing your

thoughts and feelings create a firm foundation of trust and understanding. As Ecclesiastes 4:9-10 reminds us, 'Two are better than one; because they have a good reward for their labour.'

WHAT TO DO DURING COURTSHIP

First things first, do not rush or be in haste. Many people have the mindset that they will miss out on this person and never find someone else, but it's an unhealthy perspective. When in doubt about any serious matter, please wait. We have previously discussed that marriage should not be entered hastily.

You might be wondering if the Bible provides a detailed guide for courtship. Although the Bible may not offer a step-by-step guide, it is filled with valuable insights and instructions that can be applied to various aspects of our lives, including relationships. The scriptures offer us precious revelations and directives that illuminate the path we should follow.

Because cultural and historical contexts in biblical times differed significantly from contemporary ideas of courtship, we do not see many examples of courting couples. Through scripture, the couple we see during their courtship is Joseph courtship/and Mary, because of the Israelite culture which allowed for arranged marriages. This is not to say there were no courtships in those days. I believe Jacob and Rachael could have had a friendly relationship even before he paid her Bride Price through his years of labour in Laban's house. Ruth and Boaz may not have had a lengthy courtship, but they still had one. The period between the interactions in his field and his proposal to the elders at the gate was a time of knowing each other. Within that time, they had examined themselves and most likely sought God over their decisions.

- Submit to Family and Appropriate Authority
With courtship, you need to involve your families in the process and communicate openly about your relationship. Do not keep it a secret! Let your families know you are involved with each other. By including them in your journey, you are showing

respect for their place in your life, building trust, and creating room for guidance and much needed support. Moreso, their insight and blessings can bring an extra layer of joy and wisdom. I do not agree that there should be any such thing as a secret courtship. This is not the time for secrecy. Otherwise, you will set yourself up for disaster.

The reason some couples desire hidden courtship is that they fear their families will not approve of their chosen partner. It is however, important to recognise that families many times offer valuable insights you do not see. On the other hand, there are instances where families may reject a potential spouse for the wrong reasons. That is why the first and most important step is prayer and committing the relationship to God.

I remember facing a similar fear within my family because of their strict warnings against marrying outside of the Urhobo tribe. When I mustered the courage and expressed my desire to marry Ebunoluwa, my parents vehemently refused because she was not Urhobo. The ancestral rule in our clan emphasized marrying within our tribe, and I was well aware of this. My parents made it clear that if I persisted in choosing Ebunoluwa, they would no longer fund my education. It was not an empty threat; they were steadfast in their decision and followed through on their words. However, as a man of strong convictions, I knew that if God had spoken to me about her; I had to follow those convictions regardless of the consequences.

Now Boaz went up to the gate and sat down there; and behold, the close relative of whom Boaz had spoken came by. So Boaz said, "Come aside, friend, sit down here." So he came aside and sat down. 2 And he took ten men of the elders of the city, and said, "Sit down here." So they sat down. 3 Then he said to the close relative, "Naomi, who has come back from the country of Moab, sold the piece of land which belonged to our brother Elimelech. 4 And I thought to inform you, saying, Buy it back in the presence of the inhabitants and the elders of my people. If you will redeem it, redeem it; but if you will not redeem it, then tell me, that I may know; for there is no one but you to redeem it, and I am next after you.' "And he said, "I will redeem it." 5 Then Boaz said, "On the day you buy the field from the hand of Naomi, you must also buy it from Ruth the Moabitess, the wife of the dead, to perpetuate the name of the dead through his inheritance." 6 And the close relative said, "I cannot redeem it for myself, lest I ruin my own inheritance. You redeem my right of redemption for yourself, for I cannot redeem it." 7 Now this was the custom in former times in Israel concerning redeeming and exchanging, to confirm anything: one man took off his sandal and gave it to the other, and this was a confirmation in Israel. 8 Therefore the close relative said to Boaz, "Buy it for yourself." So he took off his sandal. 9 And Boaz said to the elders and all the people, "You are witnesses this day that I have bought all that was Elimelech's, and all that was Chilion's and Mahlon's, from the hand of Naomi. 10 Moreover, Ruth the Moabitess, the widow of Mahlon, I have acquired as my wife, to perpetuate the name of the dead through his inheritance, that the name of the dead may not be cut off from among his brethren and from his position at the gate. You are witnesses this day." 11 And all the people who were at the gate, and the elders, said, "We are witnesses. The LORD make the woman who is coming to your house like Rachel and Leah, the two who built the house of Israel; and may you prosper in Ephrathah and be famous in Bethlehem. (Ruth 4:1-11) NKJV

Involving families in the decision-making process is the biblical standard. Take the story of Boaz, for example. Even after Ruth approached him on the threshing floor, he went to the elders and her family. Similarly, Abraham's servant, when tasked with finding a wife for Isaac, promptly approached Rebekah's family (Genesis 24:50-53). Jacob also went to Laban, Rachael's father (Genesis 29:13-20). Scripture offers many examples of involving families in courtship.

So, my brother, my sister, do not be afraid; have faith in God. If He has spoken to you about that relationship, trust in His word and involve your family. Remember, anything done without faith is sin (Romans 14:23). Involving family usually leads to a better outcome. The idea of a secret courtship, where only the two individuals are involved, creates room for sin and other negative consequences. I have seen this happen time and again, so I know that it is possible to be with someone who is living a lie without your knowledge. So, let both families be involved, to ensure transparency and prevent potential problems.

- Submit to Godly Counsel
Throughout the journey of a relationship, it is crucial toseek and embrace God's counsel. You will find His infinite wisdom in the Scriptures; through prayer and studying His word. (Proverbs 3:5-6). You also need to seek the counsel of spiritual authority, and those who are older in the faith and experience, because they can offer valuable perspectives and understanding based on their own experiences that which, by God's grace, they are already living out. They can provide perspectives that go beyond our own limited understanding, and share divine wisdom gained by the grace of God from their own life experiences. As we turn to spiritual authorities,

experienced individuals, and older believers, we gain valuable insights and understanding have that transcend our perspectives.

- Seek ample counsel, especially from trusted and mature Christians who have showed a strong and vibrant faith and character who will see beyond what you see. Proverbs 15:22 states that 'without counsel purposes are disappointed: but in the multitude of counsellors, they are established'.

- Recognising leadership from church authority, pastors, mentors, and elders is of utmost importance, and it is essential for the couple to be open and submitted to their counsel throughout the entire process.

Don't wait until your plans are completed; involve them from the early stages to benefit from their support and guidance. As a Pastor, I have had the privilege of counselling many intending couples, and as a result, I have witnessed diverse responses. We have counselled some intending couples who received our guidance and found joy in successful marriages, while others have been rescued from detrimental relationships, literally snatched out of fire. Unfortunately, there are those who have responded with anger, slander, and some even left the church. Nonetheless, I encourage you to respond positively to godly counsel regarding your relationship.

The way of a fool is right in his own eyes, But he who heeds counsel is wise. (Proverbs 12:15) NKJV

- Plan your Future Together
I believe this is one of the most crucial aspects of your courtship. Plan your future as a builder plans the house he intends to build.

For which of you, intending to build a tower,
does not sit down first and count the cost,
whether he has enough to finish it—
(Luke 14:28) NKJV

The most important part of this project is the foundation, and the Bible also says, 'If the foundations be destroyed, what can the righteous do?' Your foundation as a couple should be rooted in a shared purpose. The Biblical purpose for life is to fulfil God's purpose for us. If we are to partner with someone for life, our purposes must align. As a lady, how can you be a helpmeet to someone whose goal in life is far from yours? Dear brother in Christ, how do you lead a sister who can neither see nor believe in the direction that the Lord has shown you? When you have established that you are heading in the same direction, you plan how to get there. Plan together. Plan realistically. And plan in faith.

Beyond the plan, begin laying the foundation. The point of planning is this: as you get into marriage, if you veer off course, you know that the building is not going as designed, and you can correct it. Marriage is not a sandcastle; it is a towering skyscraper, have this in mind while you plan.

It is important to have open and honest conversations about your individual purposes and seek God's guidance in aligning them. What do you see? Both of you must see the same picture. It must not have identical lines and strokes, but the canvass must be the same, and the colours and shades will need to be harmonious. Discuss your aspirations, hopes and dreams. By doing this, you create an opportunity to explore the depths of each other's souls and find unity with God's grand design.

Discuss your financial plan. What are your plans for ensuring the well-being and security of your family? Will your wife work a corporate job? Have conversations about her career aspirations and goals. How many children do you want to have? What city will you live in? Also, discuss possible eventualities: what happens when one person has to leave foanother city for employment? You are about to enter a life contract with another person, and you can never over-plan for this.

Agree on critical issues in marriage, such as having children, where you will raise your family, what kind of family setting you will want your home to have - whether nuclear or extended etc. Sure, circumstances may eventually change, and these answers may not be the outcome, but it helps to know the other person's perspective. As a lady, if you have a strong desire to have children and envision motherhood as a significant part of your life, it is crucial to express this and make sure your partner shares the same sentiment. So, you do not get a sshlck in marriage discovering that your husband 8does not want children and would rather keep a pet.

Talk and talk a lot! Talk about everything, you will be amazed at how much you can learn about a person from conversing with them. The more you converse with someone, the more you learn about their passions, dreams, fears, and aspirations. Talk about the healthcare plan. (Yes, I know you walk by faith, but you need to be open about what issues require joint faith and prayers). Where necessary, talk about cultural backgrounds, traditions, and customs, family dynamics, relatives, and in-laws. And listen. Listen a lot and pay keen attention to details.

As you have these conversations, you may disagree on certain aspects. This is typical. Strive to know what areas you agree on; know your points of disagreement and how to find a middle ground. You must be wise in the way you respond to disagreements; be willing to make some compromises. When you disagree, do it without being critical of the other person, for the Bible says:

"[Love] bears all things, believes all things, hopes all things, endures all things."
(1 Corinthians 13:7) NKJV

I look back and I remember the countless hours Ebunoluwa and I spent in deep conversations. Communication formed the bedrock of our relationship, and its value became evident over time as it forged a profound bond of friendship between us.

- Building the Bond of Friendship
If you plan to spend the rest of your life with someone, it should be someone with whom you are friends. Love is built upon a strong foundation of friendship. Your spouse is someone to play and laugh with, someone you enjoy spending quality

time with. Ebun found me funny and enjoyable to be around, and it significantly boosted my confidence. She brought me peace and tranquillity. My serene sanctuary - I could easily envision a future with her as not just a romantic partner, but also as a dear friend and sister.

Focus on building a strong friendship rather than solely pursuing romance. Because the intensity of the initial passion you experience in early romance may fade over time. When you marry your friend, you have something to hold on to, even when this passion evolves. During courtship, plant the seeds of friendship that will blossom into a flourishing marriage.

- Be Open and Honest
The period of courtship is the time to be completely honest. If this is the person you are planning to spend the rest of your life with, honesty and trust are non-negotiable. Open up any hidden thing in the past that you have not mentioned until now. (Ephesians 4:25) NIV:

Therefore, each of you must put off falsehood and speak truthfully to your neighbour, for we are all members of one body.

Confidently and truthfully reveal anything that the other person needs to know. That is a genuine test of love and trust. Be ready to share truths, whether or not they are pleasing. It may be about past relationships, failures, or even convictions. Receive every piece of information with love, honour and respect, and if there are issues too grievous for you to bear alone, suggest counselling with a respected third party.

I had a troubled past, where I made choices that I deeply regretted. While we were only friends, I disclosed my past to Ebun, sharing stories of my escapades and mistakes I had made. I held nothing back, choosing to be completely transparent with her. I told her what I could remember! And true to her name, she handled all I told her gracefully. Except you are courting another Melchizedek, if you cannot trace the history of the person you want to marry, you are building a failure in advance.

- Neglect the Counsel of the Ungodly

Seeking godly counsel and authority, including your family's, is crucial. However, be mindful of complex situations where unreasonable opposition arises. For instance, when a person's family opposes their decision to marry a Christian based on unfounded or nonbiblical reasons. In such circumstances, seeking advice from church leadership becomes even more significant. As your relationship progresses, more and more people will give their opinion, you will also receive unsolicited opinions. If you are certain, however, that this relationship aligns with God's will, remain steadfast in your conviction. Set your face like a flint and confidently move forward, following the path He has laid before you.

My relationship with Ebunoluwa was going well until I involved my family. They were resolute in opposing the move, citing tribal differences. My mother vowed we would never marry because Ebun was not Urhobo. She seized all her photos in a bid to sever my ties with her. They threatened to stop funding my education, and my response was, "Mama, I'm going to school." During a family meeting, tensions escalated as they argued about my relationship with "someone who was not Urhobo". In the midst of the heated exchange, my grandma, in a traditional gesture of pronouncing a curse, brought out her aged breast and declared, "No strange daughter-in-law will marry into this family. Over my dead body!" The seriousness of the situation was palpable; and the tension in the room, tangible. I understood the risks involved when traditional people adamantly reject someone, and I knew Ebun was already at risk. So, I called her and explained that I needed to back out. With no details. I only let her know she might be at risk, and I did not want to endanger her. I loved her too much to do that. Though I knew what the Lord had told me, I was afraid for our future. And more worried about her.

"I love you, but I don't want you to suffer. This relationship will have to end. If you marry me and anything happens to me, you will suffer under these people." I said.

Did God speak to me? Yes, but I had never experienced that sort of ritual before. And if you come from a family as peculiar as mine, you would understand.

All she said to me that day was,

"Do you think I didn't know all these things would happen?"

"You did?" I asked in disbelief.

She said: "Yes, God told me."

"But why didn't you tell me?"

"It was not necessary." She calmly responded.

This matter became a prayer point. We engaged in intense prayer and spiritual warfare. If it was His will, He would make a way in the wilderness. We fought and ultimately prevailed.

Sometimes, people's opinions can be misguided, just like my family's perspective on my wife. Their objections were based solely on traditional grounds, but we knew that God's plan and purpose superseded any cultural norms or human reasoning. Boaz, being an established man, would have encountered opposition from his family when he chose to marry Ruth, a foreign woman. Bringing someone from an alien background would not have been well-received by his entire family. Boaz, however, was certain of God's will and had made up his mind. He stood firm in his conviction and proceeded with his intention to marry Ruth, despite any potential consequences or disapproval from others. Indeed, Ruth's background as a Moabitess and her conversion to Judaism might have presented challenges from the understanding of Jewish customs. Yet, Boaz looked beyond these differences and saw something remarkable in her — a teachable spirit and genuine submission to her mother-in-law, Naomi.

PRAYER

Dear Heavenly Father, I commit my relationship with [Fiancé (e)'s Name] to you. Help us strengthen the foundation of our love, rooted in faith and friendship. I ask you to lead and guide us as we plan our future, aligning our goals with your kingdom purpose. Grant us wisdom to seek godly counsel, remain open and honest, and build our relationship based on trust. Protect us from ungodly influences and opposition, and help us stand firm in our commitment. May our courtship bring glory and praise to you. In Jesus' name, I pray. Amen.

ACTION POINTS

1. **Involve Families and Appropriate Authority:** Make it a priority to involve your families and spiritual authorities in the decision-making process. Communicate openly with them about your relationship and seek their insights, blessings, and guidance. Recognise that involving families is the biblical standard and leads to better outcomes.

2. *Plan Your Future Together*: Create a shared vision for your future as a couple. Plan together, discuss aspirations, career goals, financial plans,

family size, and potential challenges that may arise. Ensure your individual purposes align with God's greater purpose for your lives. Openly communicate about critical issues.

3. **Build the Bond of Friendship**: Prioritise building a strong friendship. Spend quality time together, enjoying each other's company, and cultivating a deep bond of trust, respect, and companionship.

CHAPTER ELEVEN

PURITY AND
SANCTIFICATION

Marriage is honourable among all, and the bed undefiled; but fornicators and adulterers God will judge. (Hebrews 13:4) NKJV

PURITY
We will spend some time discussing purity because it is critical, and the Bible has so much to say on the topic. It is important to mention that Ruth and Boaz did not engage in premarital sex. The Bible provides clear and detailed information about various aspects of their relationship, and we find in the fourth chapter that they had sexual relations only after they got
married. Scripture records she lay at his feet until morning that night on the threshing floor.

The word of God unequivocally sets forth the standards for sexual purity. Sex is only permitted in marriage. In line with the teachings of Hebrews 13:4, we are instructed to sanctify our bodies, treat others' bodies with dignity, and demonstrate reverence for God through our sexuality.

For ye know what commandments we gave you
by the Lord Jesus. For this is the will of God,
 even your sanctification, that ye should abstain
from fornication: That every one of you should
know how to possess his vessel in sanctification
and honour; Not in the lust of concupiscence,
even as the Gentiles which know not God: That
no man go beyond and defraud his brother in
any matter: because that the Lord is the avenger
of all such, as we also have forewarned you
and testified. For God hath not called us unto
uncleanness, but unto holiness.
(1 Thessalonians 4:2-8).

In our current culture, premarital sex is becoming increasingly popular, blurring the lines between so-called Christian relationships and those of unbelievers. They walk like them, talk like them, dress like them, and engage in the same immoral practices. These things should not even be mentioned among us!

But among you there must not be even a hint
of sexual immorality, or of any kind of impurity
(Ephesians 5:3) NIV

Having a shared understanding of what behaviours align with our faith is crucial in any relationship. That is why having an agreement on scripture and the principles of the word of God matter. If you and your beloved are not on the same page regarding your convictions about premarital sex, then you have an issue on your hands. You must hold tight to your convictions, this is not being legalistic; it is simply living according to the unchanging standard of God's word.

You are to abstain from... sexual immorality.
(Acts 15:29) NIV

Sexual intimacy has a purpose. It is holy and honourable before the Lord. But it remains an exclusive reserve for married. couples. This is not about being old-fashioned. The word of God abides forever. He wants us to experience the beauty of intimacy in the right context and at the right time. God does not deny us pleasure; instead, He is reserving it for the right time.

As Harold S. Martin rightly puts it in The Five C's of Christian Courtship:

There are many dangers and pitfalls for young people
during the years of courtship. The devil stands ready to
lead you into sin and to spoil the happiness of your life.
God has made the bodies of men and women so that they
attract each other. Woven into the physical bodies of both
boys and girls are certain natural sex functions. These

are necessary for the reproduction of the human race, but
sex experience is right only within the bounds of true and
honourable marriage.

A woman is uniquely created, sealed with the Producer's seal, meant to be broken only on the wedding night. This consummates the marriage and establishes a covenant.

This covenant is sacred and remains binding until death, as expressed in the wedding vows, 'till death do us part'. In this context, sexual intercourse is the ultimate consummation of a marriage, holding greater significance than formalities, like signing a register, exchanging rings, or partaking in Holy Communion at the church ceremony.

Therefore, as a Christian, you should not enter such a covenant with anyone you do not intend to keep the contract with for the rest of your life, even if you are engaged to be married.

SANCTIFICATION

If one finds themselves in a situation where a covenant has been broken or made in error, there is still hope and redemption through another blood covenant, that of God's son, Jesus Christ. This covenant covers and forgives all that has been uncovered and breaks covenants that were made amiss. It is essential to recognise that God takes covenants seriously, and the blood of His son brings us a more efficacious covenant if you go to Him. If you have compromised your boundaries in your courtship and broken the hedge, it is never too late to make a change. Set new boundaries and trust in the Lord to grant you the grace and strength to uphold them. The sacrifice of Jesus Christ and His shed blood have the power to cleanse our conscience from past mistakes and actions. Hebrews 9:14 says,

How much more, then, will the blood of Christ, who through the eternal Spirit offered Himself unblemished to God, cleanse our consciences from acts that lead to death, so that we may serve the living God!

Indeed, when we come to him in repentance and accept his new covenant, we are set free from every evil covenant of our past. So, I say to you, tu)away from your past and accept this new life!

TAKING HEED
During courtship, it is crucial to take precautions and avoid overconfidence solely based on being Christians. Temptation is ever-present, so the Bible does not advise casual approaches to fornication; instead, it admonishes us to flee from it. (1Cor 6:18) Steer clear of any behaviour that will lead to sexual sin. It does not matter if you are already engaged to be married the next day; if it is not within the confines of marriage, it is a sin.

If you want to avoid sexual intercourse, here are some things to steer clear of.

1. **Do not kiss each other:** This is usually the first step in the journey to further physical intimacy.

Why start a journey
you do not wish to end?
2. Do not sit on each other's laps.

3. Avoid staying indoors alone for long periods, as it may heighten temptation.
4. Avoid being alone in isolated places at odd hours.
5. Do not sleep in the same bed.
6. Do not undress around each other.
7. Do not engage in sexting or sending explicit messages that may encourage sexual thoughts or actions.

These are not meant to stifle the freedom of lovers, but to preserve the gift of intimacy for themselves. True and meaningful intimacy can be achieved without engaging in sexual activities. The fleeting and sinful pleasures of fornication rob people of the true essence of sex, preventing them from enjoying its beauty and benefits within the context of marriage. Sex is incredibly beautiful when it is not perverted. However, when expressed in lust and lack of self-control, it can become an inferno that consumes even the very best of us.

I often wonder, how can we be certain that a person who lacks self-control in fornication will exercise self-control in marriage and resist adultery? Lust is lust, regardless of the context or circumstances. Whether it occurs outside of marriage in fornication or within marriage in adultery, it is the same spirit. When you do not learn self-control in a relationship, it will be more difficult to manifest it in marriage. As a believer, you must keep your guard up and resist all forms of temptation, flee every appearance of evil and walk in obedience to God's Word, seeking His grace and strength to uphold purity.

It is not old-fashioned to maintain high standards of purity. The fleeting thrill and exhilaration that comes with the anticipation of the forbidden, 'stolen waters' as the Bible calls it, is not worth the guilt and sin that follows afterwards.

As a young man in a relationship, see the lady first as your sister. Consider the story of Ruth and Boaz, where he had a golden opportunity when she came to him on the threshing floor. Boaz chose not to make any advances towards her. Despite being a vulnerable young lady at the feet of a powerful man, he did not take advantage of her vulnerability. Rather, he felt fear, not lust.

May our generation of men be filled with the fear of God, and may they treat vulnerable women with utmost respect, never taking undue advantage of them. Boaz woke up in the night and saw Ruth lying at his feet. The Bible states, "It came to pass that the man was afraid, and turned himself, and behold a woman laid at his feet." She was in a position of submission, totally trusting him, yet he did not take advantage of her vulnerability.

Pastor Chris Loose of Rabat International Church in his sermon on Ruth's proposal, says:
Despite the risks, Ruth came to Boaz on the threshing

floor and made herself completely vulnerable to him. She
put herself in his hands and what happened to her would
be completely up to him. She could be treated as a one-
night conquest. She could be rejected as a woman of loose
morals. She let down her defences and waited to see how
Boaz would treat her.

She chose to trust him as a righteous man, and her decision paid off. Unfortunately, many other sisters were not as fortunate as Ruth. Some decided to trust a brother or mentor, only to be taken advantage of in return. If the person you wish to marry cannot control their emotions and sexual desires before marriage, what makes you think they will control them in marriage?

I vividly recall a situation when a lady came to my office for counselling. I had no idea she had feelings for me. As we spoke, she made comments like, "I love the way you talk" and "I love the way you move your eyes." Since she was a friend's daughter, I did not think much of it initially. However, when I eventually realised that she was propositioning me, I did not pretend or ignore it. I immediately gave her a stern warning and, without hesitation, ran for my life, avoiding any potential complications. I did not fake it. I ran for my life. My brother, if you ever find yourself in a similar situation, I urge you to run for your life too.

In Ruth 3:10, Boaz referred to Ruth as his daughter.

Then he said, "Blessed are you of the LORD, my daughter! For you have shown more kindness at the end than at the beginning, in that you did not go after young men, whether poor or rich. (Ruth 3:10) NKJV

Young man, the woman you want to marry is first of all your daughter, your sister, and your friend. She is not a sex toy or an object of satisfaction; she is family. You are expected to protect her as you would your sister. Young lady, the man you intend to spend your life with should be seen as your brother, pastor, father, and friend. Please do not put him in a difficult situation; be supportive and help him stand strong, ensuring he does not fall on your account. Building a relationship based on respect for one another's purity and sanctification is key to a healthy and fulfilling marriage.

PRAYER
Dear Heavenly Father, I commit my relationship with [Fiancé (e)'s name] to you. We submit ourselves to you, spirit, soul, and body.

We come before you, recognising our human weaknesses and the temptations that surround us. Lord, we receive your grace to abstain from sexual sin.

Fill us with your Holy Spirit, so that we will resist the desires of the flesh and honour you with our bodies. We trust in your grace and keep us on the right path and to live according to your Word.

I decree and declare that sin has no place in our bodies, and we glorify You with our bodies. In Jesus' name, we pray. Amen.

ACTION POINTS

Practice Purity and Sanctification: Abstain from sexual immorality!

CHAPTER TWELVE

HOW LONG IS
TOO LONG?

"There is a time for everything, and a season for every activity under the heavens: a time to be born and a time to die, a time to plant and a time to uproot, a time to kill and a time to heal, a time to tear down and a time to build, a time to weep and a time to laugh, a time to mourn and a time to dance, a time to scatter stones and a time to gather them, a time to embrace and a time to refrain from embracing. a time to seek, and a time to lose; a time to keep, and a time to cast away; (Ecclesiastes 3:1-6) NIV

Courtship is not forever, but it is not a sprint either. Understanding a person takes a considerable amount of time, and indeed, it may take a lifetime to truly know someone. While courting for a lifetime is not practical, I would recommend a courtship period that is not too short. It is not merely about how long you have known a person, but how well you know them, and that requires time. You cannot genuinely know someone overnight. Even after many years of marriage, I am still discovering new aspects of my wife. So, avoid rushing; take the time to make discoveries. As Proverbs 20:25 (NIV) wisely says, "It is a trap to dedicate something rashly and only later to consider one's vows." Allow the relationship to grow and deepen gradually, fostering a strong foundation for a lasting and meaningful connection.

Study the person like a book; people take time to reveal their true nature. But at the same time, I would not advise an overly long courtship period. The key is not just how long you have known the person, but how well you know them. Would you like to put your life, entire being and destiny in the hands of someone you do not know well enough? Taking the time to know someone well before making such significant commitments is crucial for building a strong and meaningful relationship based on trust and mutual understanding.

After a considerable amount of time spent getting to know each other, you are likely to have enough information to assess your compatibility and suitability for marriage. At this point, it becomes crucial not to waste any more time, but to make a thoughtful and well-informed decision about your future.

In human relations, it is said that "the proof of the pudding is in the eating." The purpose of a relationship is to determine its suitability for marriage. After investing time and effort, you'll gain valuable insights. If it is not a good fit, you'll likely sense it, and if things aren't working, you'll also recognise the signs. My brother, my sister, do not deceive yourselves or prolong uncertainty when the evidence is clear. Make a decisive choice based on what you have learned, as there is no benefit in forcing if things do not work.

WHEN COURTSHIP DOES NOT WORK
Courtship is not marriage. Think of it as a dress

rehearsal. A time to make final adjustments and evaluations before taking the next step. Unfortunately, some people do not bother to re-evaluate their decision because they are primarily preoccupied with their wedding preparation, which can be a mistake. Even when you are engaged, if you notice anything that raises doubts in your mind, do not sweep it under the carpet; address it.

I believe in weighing compatibility for the long haul. So, suppose your courtship does not work in the end; glory to God! It means you have proved that it would not work out for the two of you in marriage and, in my opinion, that is a positive outcome. If you have found out that you are incompatible, it is best to end the courtship. There is no sense in wasting time, hoping against hope, forcing things to go well, wondering what people will say, hoping that things will sort themselves out. As the saying goes, *"It is better to have a broken relationship than to end up with a broken marriage."*

Look beyond the now, and consider the bigger picture:

Think about the long-term implications. Will the doubts you have now affect your happiness and well-being in the future?

Observe the signs of things you cannot tolerate in a person. People do not change overnight, so if there are major issues in someone's life that you do not want to see in your marriage, it is best to walk away while you still have the chance. Some things are absolutely too important to gamble on.

Even an engagement can be broken if you observe troubling signs. Signs act as pointers to a destination, and if the signs you see indicate a path you do not want to travel, it is crucial to take a detour and save yourself from an avoidable crash in the future. My brother, my sister, insisting on a relationship that is not working, is like seeing a sign that says 'road closed' – you do not drive through and hope for the best.

The word of God gives us essential guidance in this area. It's not just about how long you've been together, but how well you truly know each other. Ecclesiastes 3:1 reminds us that there is a time for everything. Courtship should be a time to grow, learn, and develop a bond that will withstand the challenges of marriage. If you are not growing, or learning, or developing a bond, you need to have a rethink.

Trust your instincts and have the courage to make the right decisions for your well-being and happiness. It is better to address potential concerns early on rather than risk a future full of regrets and heartache. The goal is for both parties to emerge emotionally unharmed, whether the courtship leads to marriage or not.

PRAYER

Dear Lord, teach us to number our days, that we may apply our hearts unto wisdom. (Psalm 90:12).

ACTION POINTS

1. **Address Doubts**: If doubts or concerns arise during courtship, do not ignore or suppress them.

2. **End Incompatible Courtships**: End it now.

CHAPTER THIRTEEN

MARRIAGE

Therefore, shall a man leave his father and his mother, and shall cleave unto his wife: and they shall be one flesh. (Genesis 2:24b)

And he answered and said unto them, Have ye not read, that he which made them at the beginning made them male and female, And said, For this cause shall a man leave father and mother, and shall cleave to his wife: and they twain shall be one flesh? Wherefore they are no more twain, but one flesh. What therefore God hath joined together, let not man put asunder. (Matt 19:4-6)

After the encounter on the threshing floor, Boaz could not help but be driven to resolve the matter at hand. I can picture him pacing back and forth on the threshing floor, for the rest of the morning contemplating how he could marry the young lady, knowing full well that he was not the first in the line among the relatives. Boaz must have been a man of prayer, and as with all other matters before, he brought this before Jehovah, asking for his goodness and favour. Unknown to him, the Lord had gone ahead.

So Boaz took Ruth and she became his wife. (Ruth 4:13)

First, Boaz was eager to find out if the closer kinsman, who had the first right to redeem Ruth, would take her as his wife. I believe he secretly hoped that the kinsman would decline, as Ruth had already captured his heart.

As it turned out, the closer kinsman seemed to be more interested in taking advantage of the situation. He jumped at the idea of acquiring a widow's property, seeing it as a profitable opportunity. His assumption was that a poor widow would be desperate to sell, and he could take advantage of her situation. However, when he learned the deal required him to redeem the widow Ruth as well, he swiftly changed his mind. Taking on the responsibility of marrying Ruth and fulfilling the duty of a kinsman-redeemer was too much for him to handle, and he promptly declined the offer. His true intentions of seeking personal gain were exposed, and he chose to step away from the situation.

Then he said to the close relative, "Naomi, who has come back from the country of Moab, sold the piece of land which belonged to our brother Elimelech. And I thought to inform you, saying, Buy it back in the presence of the inhabitants and the elders of my people. If you will redeem it, redeem it; but if you will not redeem it, then tell me, that I may know; for there is no one but you to redeem it, and I am next after you.' "

And he said, "I will redeem it." Then Boaz said, "On the day you buy the field from the hand of Naomi, you must also buy it from Ruth the Moabitess, the wife of the dead, to perpetuate the name of the dead through his inheritance."

And the close relative said, "I cannot redeem it for myself, lest I ruin my own inheritance. You redeem my right of redemption for yourself, for I cannot redeem it." (Ruth 4:3-6) NKJV

The guy ran off! Likely seeing Ruth as a liability and wanting no responsibility. He only wanted the gains and benefits without being willing to bear any burdens or cover her. Marriage is a partnership; it is about bearing one another up. Be cautious of people who only want your substance but are unwilling to bear your burdens with you. In Boaz's case, he gladly accepted Ruth, along with all that she came with,

He said: *"I will purchase the property and redeem the widow along with it."*

JESUS, OUR REDEEMER

This is a type of our redemption story. Although Jesus was rich, He became poor for our sake. He married us into His family, carrying our weights with Him and redeeming us from the penalty of our sins. Just like Ruth, we were once poor and wretched, foreigners with nothing to offer but our love, submission, and wholehearted commitment to Him. Jesus embraced us in all our brokenness and flaws, demonstrating His unconditional love and grace.

In contemplating the beautiful story of Ruth and Boaz, we find a powerful reflection of our redemption through Jesus Christ, our ultimate Kinsman Redeemer. As the New Testament proclaims, Jesus is the groom, and the Church is His beloved bride. Through His immense love and sacrifice, He willingly chose to become poor for our sake, leaving the riches of heaven to walk among us. Just as Boaz married Ruth into his family, Jesus has chosen to unite us with Himself, redeeming us from the chains of sin and granting us the hope of eternal life. He bore the weight of our transgressions, carrying our burdens upon His shoulders, and paying the price for our sins through His own blood.

In doing so, He demonstrated the depths of His unconditional love and grace for each one of us.

Like Ruth, we were once poor and wretched, without any merit to offer. Yet, Jesus willingly embraced us in our brokenness, taking us as we are with all our baggage, and transforming us into His chosen people, His cherished bride. Through His redemption, we find restoration, forgiveness, and the promise of eternal life in His glorious presence.

So, let us marvel at this redemption story, where the rich and perfect Saviour humbled Himself to become one with the poor and undeserving. In His infinite love, He calls us His own and purchases us into the eternal family of God. As His redeemed, we can walk with confidence and hope, knowing that we are forever cherished and secure in the arms of our beloved Kinsman Redeemer, Jesus Christ.

Absolutely! Just as Ruth found refuge and redemption at Boaz's feet on the threshing floor, we too can come to Jesus with open hearts and find forgiveness, love, and a place in His eternal family.

If you haven't yet given your heart to the Lord, know that He eagerly awaits to embrace you with His arms of grace and shelter you under His loving wings.

If you have not given your heart to the Lord and desire to begin this transformative journey with Jesus, you can say this prayer from your heart:

"Lord Jesus, I come to You and lay myself at Your feet. I recognise that I am a sinner and in need of Your forgiveness. Please cleanse me from all my sins and redeem me into Your precious family. I surrender my life to You and ask that You become the Lord of my heart and my Saviour. Thank You for Your immense love and grace. Amen."

Know that in saying this prayer sincerely, you open the door for Jesus to enter your life, transform you, and begin a new lineage of grace with you. Embrace this divine invitation and rest assured that you are now a beloved member of God's family, forever united with your loving Kinsman Redeemer, our Lord Jesus Christ.

REFERENCES

• Hitz, Shelley. (2016). Broken Crayons Still Colour. Body and Soul Publishing.

• Yitzchai, Schlomo. (Rashi). (2003). Jeremiah 2. Sefaria.org. https://www.sefaria.org/Jeremiah.7.31?lang=bi&with=all&lang2=en

• Wright, Norman. H. (2000). The Perfect Catch. Bethany House. pages 28-29

• Prince, Derek. (2006). Blessing or Curse, You Can Choose. Chosen books. p 104

• Smedes, Lewis. Benedictus. Fancy quotes. https://www.google.com/search?q = Lewis + Benedictus + Smedes + to + forgive + is + to + set + a + prisoner + free + and + discover + that + the + prisoner + was + you. & client=

• Martin, Harold. S. (Nov, 1982). The Five C's of Christian Courtship. biblehelpsinc.org. https://biblehelpsinc.org/publication/the-five-cs-of-christian-courtship/